Praise for *A Legacy that Lasts*

"Everyone ends up somewhere, but few people end up somewhere on purpose. In her new book, *A Legacy That Lasts*, Trudy Cathy White gives readers valuable tools to help them intentionally invest in their families. Packed with spiritual truth, personal examples, and doable action steps, this book will help readers clearly define their family values and pass them on to future generations."

> — **CRAIG GROESCHEL,** pastor of Life.Church
> and *New York Times* bestselling author

"When our time on earth comes to a close, those who follow will turn to what we leave behind: our legacy. *A Legacy that Lasts* contains intentional tools to cultivate your family values today and inspire generations tomorrow. A timely read for any stage of life!"

> — **DR. TONY EVANS,** president of The Urban
> Alternative and senior pastor of Oak Cliff Bible
> Fellowship

"With adult children and a budding generation of grandchildren, Willie and I find ourselves returning more and more to the topic of legacy in our home. This book is right on time for us and for any family that understands the importance of passing on God-honoring family values. I am so grateful to Trudy for sharing such personal stories and helpful tools so that we can go about building a beautiful legacy for the future generations!"

> — **KORIE ROBERTSON,** Duck Dynasty and
> author of *Strong and Kind*

"The way we live out our days will shape the legacy of our lives. Trudy has done this for her own family and will be a faithful guide as you build a vision for your family that will make a difference in the generations to come."

> — **JENNIE ALLEN,** New York Times bestselling
> author of *Find Your People and Get Out of Your
> Head*, founder and visionary of IF:Gathering

A Legacy that Lasts

A Legacy that Lasts

PRESERVING *and* TRANSFERRING YOUR FAMILY VALUES

TRUDY CATHY WHITE

daughter of Jeannette and S. Truett Cathy, founder of

Forefront
BOOKS

A Legacy that Lasts: Preserving and Transferring Your Family Values

Copyright © 2023 by Trudy Cathy White

Library of Congress Control Number: 2022911999

Print ISBN: 978-1-63763-111-9
E-book ISBN: 978-1-63763-112-6

Cover Design by Bruce Gore, Gore Studio, Inc.
Interior Design by Bill Kersey, KerseyGraphics

To our grandchildren:

Ashlynn, Anna Kathryn, Caleb, Daniel, Micah, Lydia, Reese, Wheeler, Maran, Levi, Michael, Tucker, Kaitlyn, Landon, Brooklyn, and any others God chooses to gift our family.

May you point others to Jesus as living examples of our family values.

He is the legacy that lasts.

In loving memory of Carter, our grandson in heaven, who was carried for a moment but will be loved for a lifetime.

TABLE OF CONTENTS

Acknowledgments

Two decades ago, I set a goal for myself: write one book before my mother departs this earth. Even after achieving that goal in 2004 with *Along the Way*, I didn't see myself as an author. Without the encouragement, support, and guidance from the people below, I wouldn't have considered writing subsequent books...let alone four!

My biggest champion continues to be my husband and life partner, John. That is especially true for this book. John was the inspiration behind the project and—thankfully—he didn't stop there. You'll find his fingerprints throughout as he attended writing sessions, contributed thoughts, and helped with revisions. I'm beyond thankful for his encouragement and support.

Our children and grandchildren deserve recognition as they provided abundant source material through the lives they're living, a reflection of our family values. I'm so grateful for each one of you. Thank you especially to the grandchildren who humored me with interviews and questions.

I am eternally grateful for the legacy lived by my parents, Truett and Jeannette Cathy, providing a foundation for our family—and therefore this book—to build on. I constantly learn from their example and pray I've communicated the tools given to me in a way that enables others to pass on their own legacy. Thank you also to Chick-fil-A for carrying my father's vision by "Winning Hearts Every Day." The company's commitment to uphold the Corporate Purpose and continue the legacy of our family business is a gift beyond measure. Thank you to our executive leadership, Operators, Support Center staff, and Team Members worldwide.

Last, but certainly not least, thank you to Allen Harris, who partnered with me for this third project. Allen has a way of getting in my head and putting my words into writing better than I ever thought possible. Allen and I owe a special thank you to Operator Murray Collier and the wonderful Team Members at the Spring Hill, Tennessee, Chick-fil-A who provided an inspirational workspace (and an endless supply of iced tea) for Allen to read, review, and refine this book. Likewise, special thanks to our editorial team and to Forefront Books, who made it possible for you to hold a copy of this book in your hands.

Finally, and most importantly, all gratitude to our God, who works through human frailty and our weakness as people, parents, and grandparents. I'm humbled by His promise of blessing to generation after generation.

CHAPTER 1

YOUR IDENTITY
IS NOT A CRISIS

"But do you know who she *really* is?" I heard a young mother say that to her little girl during my years as Camp Director at WinShape Camps for Girls at least a dozen times a summer. Parents and girls poured through the gates on Opening Day, and I was there to greet them—with a big smile on my face and a name tag on my shirt introducing me simply as "Trudy." Opening Day was always a madhouse, full of excited-but-nervous children getting one last hug from their moms and dads—who were often just as nervous as their young campers! As Director, it was my job to make everyone feel as enthused about arriving at camp as we were about having them there. I chatted with as many moms, dads, and campers as I could, greeting everyone and welcoming the girls for a wonderful week or two of adventure.

At least once or twice on each Opening Day, a parent would introduce me to their child like this: "Sweetie, this is your Camp Director, Mrs. Trudy. She's going to be with you girls while you're here this week." Then, there'd be a slight pause as the parent leaned in and said, "But do you know who she *really* is?"

The child would fumble around for a moment or two before the parent continued, "Well, you know those chicken nuggets and waffle fries you like so much? Her father is Truett Cathy, the man who invented Chick-fil-A. We've seen his picture hanging on the wall of the Chick-fil-A by our house! Isn't that cool?"

Yes, that is "cool." However, frankly, it's not something any young camper ever cared much about.

But it's something I've always cared very, very much about. My identity has always been and will always be bound to my Cathy family roots—even though my last name has been White for more than forty-five years now. I'm well into my sixties, and my parents have been gone several years at this point, but I will always be known as the daughter of Truett and Jeannette Cathy. And that's just fine with me.

I have held many, many roles throughout my life: Daughter. Sister. Chick-fil-A Operator. Wife. Mother. Missionary. Camp Director. Grandmother (or "Mimi"). Chick-fil-A Ambassador. Author. Speaker. Each of those roles tells you *something* about me—a piece of my life. But none of them alone tells you *who I am.* That is a much bigger question, and it's a question we all must answer for ourselves. And this generation, maybe more than any generation that's come before, is desperately trying to figure out who they are.

Like it or not, *who we are* is largely a reflection of *where we come from and the influence of relationships around us.* Our attitudes, faith system, habits—even some of our most basic instincts—are intrinsically tied to the values we were taught as children. Every family has values, whether they're intentional about articulating and communicating them or not. And those family values, together with God's unique design and call on our lives, shape us into the men and women we become. As we—in our roles as parents, grandparents, and individuals who are making an impact on the next generation—seek to shape the boys and girls in our lives into the men and women of God they were designed to be, we have to be mindful of the family values we are passing on to them and *how* we're passing on those values.

That's what this book is all about.

THE THREE BIG QUESTIONS OF LIFE

I have been involved in children's camps since I was a young girl myself. My husband, John, and I have raised four children of our own, and we're the extremely proud grandparents of *sixteen* remarkable grandchildren. We worked with young families in a completely different culture during our ten years as missionaries in Brazil. Plus, John and I have the wonderful honor of getting to know a new class of recent high school graduates every year as they enter the Impact 360 Institute gap year program we founded in 2006 alongside our nonprofit organization, Lifeshape, which we founded in 2003. So, as you can see, I have a lot of experience working with boys and girls from elementary school all the way up to college age. In all those years and in all those roles, I've found young people are predominantly faced with what we call the three big questions of life:

1. Who am I?
2. Why am I here?
3. Where do I belong?

These are the three questions that keep people up at night—and not only when they're young. I've spent many sleepless nights myself wrestling with one or two of these questions at different stages of my life, even well into adulthood. And, I bet, so have you.

Let's take a quick look at each key question.

Who Am I?

The Bible declares, "A good name is more desirable than great riches" (Proverbs 22:1, NIV). That is, our reputation—*who we are in the eyes of others*—is more valuable than anything we could ever buy and any amount of money we could ever have in the bank. But what is a "good name"? Where do we get it? How do we maintain it? How can we make sure our reputation reflects the God we serve?

Growing up, whenever my brothers or I would leave the house—whether it was to go to school, hang out with friends, or head out on a date—our mother would stand at the back door, hold it open for us, and say, "Have fun. And remember *who you are* and *whose you are!*"

"Remember who you are and whose you are." I must have heard that a thousand times as a girl. I can still hear my mom's sweet-but-stern voice ringing in my ears. She meant it. It was important to her that her children honor the Lord and behave in a manner that brought glory to Him. It was also important to her that we didn't do anything to embarrass our family—especially once Chick-fil-A started taking off and Dad was becoming more well known. Mom gave us freedom to grow, explore, and make mistakes, but she never let us forget that *who we are, wherever we are,* matters. Understanding who we are has the power to build up or tear down, and that's a responsibility my two brothers and I took very seriously as children—and even more seriously as adults.

When there's alignment and consistency in who we are, what we say, what we do, the values we proclaim, how we're making decisions, and how we're living our lives, we become a powerful testimony to the people around us. People notice when a man or woman "walks the talk"—and when they don't. How often have you heard community gossip or read shameful headlines about a pastor, religious leader, parent, teacher, coach, politician, celebrity, or local businessperson who's had a very public disconnect in what they say versus what they do? Families are broken, businesses fail, people are embarrassed, professionals lose their jobs, God's name is dishonored…all because they lived in a way that didn't match their values. They lost sight of who they were and whose they were.

As parents or grandparents/guardians, it can sometimes be difficult to truly get a good look at a child, to see them for who they are out in the world instead of in the safety of our own home. We pray for little glimpses into the man or woman they're becoming. A few years ago, God gave me such a glimpse at my oldest grandchild, Ashlynn. My daughter Joy had homeschooled Ashlynn all through elementary and middle school, but Ashlynn wanted to go to a "real" high school. So, they enrolled her in a local high school starting in the ninth grade. It was the first time Ashlynn had been out "on her own" in any significant way. Prior to that, she'd spent most of her time with her parents and siblings or at church. But now, she was heading into "the real world" of sorts, and we were curious how she'd react.

Now, as a proud grandmother, I knew Ashlynn was a special girl, always bright, smart, polite, caring, attentive—all the things you want to see in a child. But what would everyone else see? Would Ashlynn stay true to who we knew her to be when she was outside the protection of her parents?

Any fears or concerns were wiped away just a couple of months into the school year. Ashlynn—the "new girl" at school—was named the ninth-grade representative to the Homecoming Court. Because we're an extremely close family, there were some aunts and uncles in the crowd cheering her on as she gracefully walked onto the football field that night. Afterward, her uncle Ross Cathy gave her a big hug of congratulations. Her teacher saw this and recognized Ross as the Operator of their local Chick-fil-A, and she knew he was a member of "the" Cathy family, because the family name always gets attention in the Atlanta area. Ashlynn, however, isn't a Cathy by name; she's a Wilbanks. And her grandparents' last name is White. It turns out her teachers had no idea she was in any way connected to Chick-fil-A or our family.

The teacher asked Ashlynn how she knew Ross and the Cathy family, and Ashlynn thought nothing of it when she replied, "Oh, he's my uncle."

"Your uncle?!" the teacher replied, a bit surprised.

"Yes, ma'am. Truett Cathy was my great-grandfather. His daughter is my grandmother."

The teacher said, "Well, Ashlynn, I had no idea. Why didn't you ever say anything?"

"I don't know," Ashlynn said. "I never thought it would be that big a deal."

The following week, her teacher sent a video message to Joy and her husband, Trent, about Ashlynn. She raved about how sweet Ashlynn was, how she went out of her way to make everyone around her feel special and "seen," how she reflected the character of Jesus, how attentive she was to the needs of others, what a good student she was, and so on. Then, she said something that stood out to me: "You know, based on who she is, I guess it's no surprise to learn that she's a part of the Cathy family. She's lived up to everything I've ever heard about you all. And I especially respect the fact that she doesn't make a big deal about it. Other kids would probably lead with that!"

Of course, these insights into who your children and grandchildren are when they're outside your view are priceless. We raise them the best we can, trying to instill in them a strong sense of who they are, who God made them to be, and what our family values are, but you never really know for sure how well it's going until you get a report like this. I'm grateful for her teacher's thoughtful video. It not only gave me a glimpse into who Ashlynn really is but also reminded me how some people can get confused about who someone is just by their name. You see, many people think your name—or, in this case, a family name—gives you value. It doesn't. The opposite is true, in fact: we give *our names* value by who we show ourselves to be. Even at fourteen years old, Ashlynn knew the Cathy name didn't make her special. Rather, *who she is* and *who she shows herself to be* makes the Cathy name special! The same goes for me, my brothers, my children, my grandchildren, and all my nieces and nephews.

Again, "A good name is more desirable than great riches" (Proverbs 22:1, NIV). But that name is only as valuable as we make it. We can add to or take away from that value at any time. A good family name isn't a free pass, and a bad family name isn't a curse. Every name, good or bad, is only what *you* make it by the way you live out *who you are*.

Why Am I Here?

John and I were blessed to spend an entire decade—including most of our thirties—serving as missionaries in Brazil. We raised our children there; two of them were even born there! As I revealed in my previous book, *Climb Every Mountain*, God's call to overseas missions took me completely by surprise. He spoke to John first and then went to work on me, softening my heart for the people of Brazil and prompting my spirit to leave everything I knew and take a bold step of faith with Him. Despite my initial hesitations, God of course proved Himself faithful. He knew what He designed me to do, and He knew why I was needed *in that place at that time.* From our very first week there, I knew I was doing exactly what I was supposed to be doing.

Flash forward ten years, and I'd lost all certainty about the "Why am I here?" question. We had been back in the States for a few weeks. John had been called to an executive leadership position with the International Mission Board (IMB) of the Southern Baptist Convention, the mission organization we served under while in Brazil, and we'd traded our simple home in Brazil for a nice, new place in Richmond, Virginia. More importantly, we'd left behind the much-loved family of friends and ministry partners we'd developed there. And, as I quickly realized, I was afraid we'd left behind my very *purpose* as well.

There were two moments in that season of transition that rattled me to the core. The first was when I had to formally resign my position as a missionary from the IMB. After living the life of an international missionary for ten years—more than a quarter of my life at that point—it was difficult to "give up" that part of my identity. However, God had made His call clear to us that the next phase of our ministry would take place in Richmond, with John helping to lead the entire mission organization. As I signed the official document stating that I was no longer a missionary for the IMB, I couldn't help but wonder, *But ... where does this leave me?*

My second "identity crisis" moment happened just a couple of weeks later. Now that we were legal residents of Virginia, I had to get a new driver's license. During our years in Brazil, since I was not a citizen there, I simply kept my Georgia driver's license. I was born and raised in Georgia, I learned to drive in Georgia, I had taken my driver's test in Georgia twenty-plus years earlier, I kept my Georgia license while I went to college in Alabama, and I still had it when we moved overseas. For more than twenty years, whenever I needed to prove my *identity*, I pulled out *that* license. It may sound silly, but that little piece of plastic was a part of me. It was *mine*. And now, the nice lady at the Virginia Department of Motor Vehicles wanted to take it away from me.

"Ma'am, you'll need to surrender your old license before I can hand you your new one."

I could feel my face fall. Something in me was breaking as I meekly replied, "But ... but couldn't I just keep it? I know it isn't 'good' anymore, but I'd really like to keep it for sentimental value."

"I'm sorry, honey, but you can only have *one* driver's license. I need to destroy your Georgia license."

Tears welled up as I handed it to her. They were flowing in force when I got to the parking lot. By the time I got back in the car with John, who had been waiting for me, I was sobbing.

"What in the world happened in there?" he asked, trying to understand what was going on.

"I don't have anything that's *mine* anymore!" I cried. "I don't have any sense of purpose! Why in the world are we here? What am I supposed to do with my life now?"

That poor lady at the DMV! She had no idea what door she was unlocking simply by asking me to hand over my Georgia driver's license. But I suppose that was the last straw. It was a traumatic experience. I felt like the wind had been knocked out of me and the rug pulled out from under my feet, all at the same time. The weight of change in my life at that point felt unbearable. I truly didn't know who I was or what I was supposed to be doing with my life anymore.

That experience caused me to enter a season of deep searching, praying, experimentation, study, and exploration into exactly who and what God had made me to be. I'll unpack it a bit more in the following chapter, but that exploration led me to a newfound sense of purpose and identity that has brought laser focus to my understanding of why I'm here. While this book is primarily focused on family values, I pray you, too, will receive the added benefit of a renewed sense of purpose in your life as a spouse, parent, grandparent, or someone who has the opportunity to influence this next generation.

Where Do I Belong?

The third big question of life is one we're all intimately familiar with: Where do I belong? It's so easy to feel lost in this big, scary world, and few things unnerve us more than not knowing where we are or where we're going. That's a lesson that became all too real for me as a teenager—in Paris, of all places!

During my eleventh-grade year, I participated in a four-week "study abroad" excursion in London. We flew into and out of Paris, so we also stayed one night there. The day we arrived in Paris, our small group of students hit the town, trying to take in as much of the Parisian culture as we could in the few hours we had. The group I was with dropped our bags off at the hotel and immediately rushed out to visit the Louvre Museum. I was awestruck by the beauty all around me. One piece in particular caught my eye, and I lingered there admiring it. My friends, however, didn't linger quite as long as I did. When I turned to head to the next attraction, I realized my friends were gone. I scanned the crowd and couldn't find them. There were no teachers or chaperones anywhere. That was certainly an unsettling feeling, but I didn't worry too much. I just went back to admiring the works of art, certain I would bump into my friends soon enough.

I didn't.

After a while, with no familiar faces in sight, I felt a panic start to rise in my chest. I hurried through the room I was in, then the next, and then the next. I scoured as much of the Louvre as I could—it is a big place for a young girl from Georgia, after all—but I never saw my friends. As it was getting late in the afternoon, I decided to give up my search and return to the hotel. I assumed they'd done the same, and we'd all reconnect at the hotel. When I stepped out of the massive front door of the Louvre and onto the Paris streets, however, I had a horrible realization. We had taken a bus from the airport to the hotel, and I hadn't paid any attention at all to where we were on the drive. And, since we had hurried out of the hotel and to the Louvre using a tourist map of the city, I didn't remember the route back to the hotel. Worse, I didn't even know the *name* of the hotel! I was absolutely, positively lost—in a foreign country. And I couldn't speak French!

All I could think to do was to wander around a bit, praying I'd recognize *something*, some landmark from our walk to the museum. But I didn't. I got unsettling looks from several men and teenage boys, and I even got a few honks and hollers from men in cars passing by. I quickly turned and stared at the window decorations of the stores I was passing, trying to ignore the would-be suitors as best I could. I passed a police officer, but I was too scared to try to speak to him. I didn't know the language and couldn't tell him the name of the hotel, so I worried he'd take me away to the police station, where there'd be no chance of bumping into my friends. Finally, I passed by a bench at a busy intersection, and I immediately recognized it. I remembered driving past it on our bus ride to the hotel, and I knew the bus would most likely have to pass by this same bench on the way back to the airport the next morning. I figured that, if I just stayed here, the bus with my teachers and friends would drive past it, see me, and pick me up. But that meant actually staying out there, on that bench, overnight. I couldn't think of any other options.

I sat down and prayed, "Lord, would You protect me tonight as I stay right here?" I'd never felt so lost in my life. Honestly, I'm not sure I've ever felt that lost in the fifty years since either. It was truly terrifying to feel so disconnected from everything and everyone. I was cut off from the world I knew and loved, and the only thing I wanted at that moment was for someone to find me, to call out my name and bring me back to where I belonged.

And that's when I heard it: "Trudy! Trudy, is that you?"

I turned my head and saw my friends who I'd been with at the Louvre running toward me. "What are you doing?" they asked. "Why are you out here all by yourself?"

I explained what had happened, and we all shared a huge sigh of relief and a big hug. Then they said, "Come on, let's go back to the hotel." And we did. Believe it or not, it was just a stone's throw from where I was sitting. But I didn't recognize it. It could have been on the other side of town, for all I knew!

That question—*where do I belong?*—has haunted me several other times throughout my life: when I left home for the first time for college, when I opened and ran my own Chick-fil-A at age nineteen, when I got married and had to adjust to life as "John's wife," when we moved to Brazil, when I resigned as a missionary, when I moved back to Atlanta to be with my family for the first time in twenty years, when all my children were grown and gone, when I was faced with the opportunity to lead WinShape Camps for Girls, when I had to figure out my role in the company my father had built. Over and over in life, we're called on to take a good, hard look at not only *who* we are but *where* we are—and where we *should be*. Those are very difficult questions, and they require us to dig deep and draw on the strength, wisdom, and values we were raised with. Sadly, too many people are unprepared to face these challenges because their families never took "value training" seriously.

We can change that for our children and grandchildren.

CULTURE'S QUEST FOR IDENTITY AND PURPOSE

Those three questions—who am I? why am I here? and where do I belong?—drive us. Practically every major decision we make in life can be traced back to how we answer these three questions. We are yearning to know exactly what God has called us to do, both in the moment and with our lives as a whole. We are desperate to understand our identity and purpose, and we'll do almost anything to figure it out.

I think people—especially young people—today are lost. They're wandering around and grasping for anything to help them understand their identity. Like I did in Paris, they're desperately searching for something familiar, something they can feel connected to. However, it too often seems like they're looking in all the wrong places.

Everything is being questioned today in a way I've never seen before in my sixty-something years on earth. Every day, young people are told to question their faith, question their politics, question their orientation, question their relation-ships, question their upbringing, question American history, and even question fundamental scientific facts. People who have only ever shown love and compassion for all people are suddenly questioning whether they're actually racist and didn't know it. Men and women are now even told to question their biological gender. I know we live in a fallen world, but it is stunning to me that we've come to a place in history where someone can shout "Trust the science!" about one issue while completely discounting the biological reality of gender and ignoring the scientific proof that human life begins in the womb. Everything we thought we knew—everything my parents' generation simply took as fact—is now open for debate. And not only is it open for debate, but it seems like the baseline assumption is that everything we *thought* we knew is wrong. It feels like the world's turned upside-down. It's hard not to hear Jesus's warning to us about the terrible consequences of building a house on a foundation of sand: "The rain came down, the streams rose, and the winds blew and beat against that house, and it fell with a great crash" (Matthew 7:27, NIV). When there's no strong foundation, nothing we build will last.

That's one key reason John and I founded the Impact 360 Institute gap year program several years ago. It's a nine-month program designed specifically for new high school graduates who already have a relationship with Christ to spend the year before they enter college exploring themselves, their faith, and their purpose. We strive to help them get clarity on who they are and why they're here before they head off into the often confusing and challenging world of college and then the "real world." This helps them stay focused as they complete their degree programs and enter the workforce as the mature, Christ-following, grounded leaders we need right now.

THE MISSION: TO DEFINE, PRESERVE, AND TRANSFER YOUR FAMILY VALUES

Clearly, we don't want to build our children's and grandchildren's legacy on a foundation of shifting sand. But what is the strong, secure foundation we need to truly live and leave a legacy that will last for generations? I believe it is an identity and purpose built on strong, bold, specific, Bible-based family values that are not only practiced in the home but intentionally taught to our children in creative ways repeatedly throughout their entire lives—even into adulthood.

I am writing this book for one reason: to help you *define, preserve, and transfer your family values*. To do that, we'll need to go on a little journey together. Along the way, I'll explain why I think Bible-based family values are the key to raising wise, loving, giving, disciplined, God-loving boys and girls who become men and women the future so badly needs. And we won't only talk about what values are and why they matter, indeed we'll also spend a few chapters exploring creative ways you can *transfer* those values to the next generation. I'll unpack several strategies for being *intentional* about sharing your family values and show you how to create fun and memorable activities—what I call *value experiences*—that will crystalize those values in the minds of your children and/ or grandchildren. Of course, because I'm a storyteller at heart, I'll also share plenty of stories along the way from my own family's journey, giving you the chance to learn from what worked in our family... and what didn't.

Every family has family values, whether you're intentional about defining and teaching them or not. My hope is that, together, we can explore the rich landscape of family values and revolutionize how, when, where, and why they're taught. But first, we need to get a better understanding of what our values are and why they matter. We'll do that next.

CHAPTER 2

UNDERSTANDING FAMILY VALUES

In the previous chapter, we spent some time examining *who we are* and *why we're here.* Those questions speak to the deep realities of our identity—the very core of our being. Understanding our identity is crucial to living an effective, fulfilling, and enjoyable life. No one reaches the end of their life wishing they'd been *less* authentic to their true selves! Rather, we're

more likely to hear a loved one on their deathbed mournfully regret all the time they spent trying to be something and someone they weren't born to be. We are called to be *ourselves*.

The funny thing about identity is that we're actually born with *dual* identities: an identity in Christ and a family identity. We weren't created from a blank slate; no, we were knit together in the very image of God (Genesis 1:27). Moreover, Scripture declares, "My old self has been crucified with Christ. It is no longer I who live, but Christ lives in me" (Galatians 2:20, NLT). So, not only did God make us in His image, but He also *remade* us in Christ. This reminds me of a story I once heard about a little boy and his boat. This boy spent weeks painstakingly building, painting, and crafting a perfect toy boat from a model kit he'd bought with his hard-earned grass-cutting money he'd made that summer. The first time he put his boat in the river, however, the current carried it off far out of his sight. He was devastated to have lost such a precious creation. Then, months later, as he was scanning the aisles at his local toy and hobby shop, he was stunned to see a boat—*his boat*—on display. He explained to the shopkeeper that this was his boat and how he had built it then lost it.

The owner was unmoved.

"Sorry, son. I bought that from someone last week. I guess they found it on the shore. You'll have to buy it if you want it back."

The boy reached into his pocket and pulled out a wad of $1 bills—all the money he'd saved from a month's worth of cutting yards. He handed the shopkeeper the money and said, "Okay, it's worth it. I want my boat back."

As he left the shop, the child cradled his boat in his hands with the loving care of a new parent holding a baby. He whispered to the boat, "You're home now. I've got you and I won't let you go this time. I love you so much I bought you *twice*."

That's how God loves us: He loves us so much that He bought us twice—once at our birth and again in Christ. That He has marked us as *His* is a core part of our identity.

We also have a family identity, however, and that one is a bit trickier to pin down. We don't come into this world alone; we are born into a family, and that family has an identity and purpose all its own. That family identity is reflected, preserved, and transferred in the form of family values. That's how we grow to understand how a "White," a "Cathy," a "Johnson," or a "Smith" *fits* into the world around us. The family values we grow up with—whether your parents ever intentionally articulated those values or not—shape who we are as individuals and, as a result, who our children and grandchildren will become as we pass those values down generationally.

THE CASE FOR DEFINING YOUR FAMILY VALUES

The White family values are faith, family, integrity, generosity, and gratitude. If you ask me, John, or any of our four children to explain what each of these five values means and how they've been made evident in our family life for the past forty-five years, we could go on and on. In fact, I'll spend the next several chapters unpacking each of these five values and explaining why they're important to us and how they reflect our family's priorities. I'd like to say that John and I sat down early in our marriage to pray through what was important to us and what we hoped to accomplish throughout our lives in each of these five areas. I'd like to say we had these five values displayed in our home as our four children grew up. I'd like to say that from birth, all our children could recite our family values from memory at the drop of a dime. I'd love to say all those things. But I can't. The truth is, John and I were very late in getting our act together around articulating our personal and family values. Even after we discovered the sheer power in doing so—and, I'm embarrassed to say, even after we engaged a life coach to teach our then-adult children how to define *their* personal and family values—we *still* hadn't worked through the process of identifying and naming our own! If it weren't for our children's bold challenge to us, we might *still* not have taken this incredibly important step for our family.

The Values Assembly

It was the main topic of our 2011 White Family Assembly—an annual retreat for me, John, our four children, and their spouses to discuss family and business matters. (We'll discuss family assemblies later in the book.) John and I had been working with a good friend and life coach, Dr. Maurice Graham, for several years at that point, and he had recently encouraged us to start thinking more seriously about our children, the families they were starting, and the roles and responsibilities they were growing into with Chick-fil-A. Our children were in their mid-to-late twenties at that time, and Maurice rightly warned us that they were heading into a period of making some enormous life decisions. He encouraged us to help them prepare for the next phase of their lives by showing them how to set a firm foundation of clear, articulated convictions and values on which they'd base their big decisions for the rest of their lives.

Sitting around the living room of a cabin in the Blue Ridge Mountains of Georgia that weekend, Maurice introduced the concept of values to our children and their spouses. At that time, three of our four children were married. John and I listened as Maurice led lively discussions around what was important to them, what they valued in their lives, how they were raised, what they were raised to believe, and what they would use as the basis for their upcoming decisions about careers, choosing spouses, and raising children. He walked them through a process for narrowing a long list of possible values to the five that really meant the most to each of them (below I will explain the process he used). By the end of that weekend, each of our children had started thinking about a personalized list of core values that they believed represented who they were, what they believed, and where they wanted to invest their time and energy for the rest of their lives. It was an incredible experience, one we still look back on fondly more than a decade later.

Over the next several years, as we continued to meet for our family assembly retreats, we saw how committed our children were to staying value-focused in their lives. Whenever they discussed a big decision or career move, they often spoke in the context of the values they had identified in 2011. They shared how they had long discussions with their spouses about those values and what values each spouse was bringing into the marriage. They told us how they'd worked together with their spouses to identify a set of values for the new families they were creating and how they'd posted their values on the walls of their homes so they'd always be reminded of who they were as a family. They even shared how they were trying to communicate those values to the children being born and adopted into their homes. It was truly wonderful to watch our grown children take such a key concept so seriously, to know they were not leaving their family values to chance, to see how they were being proactive in becoming the men, women, and families God had called them to be.

And then, at one family assembly retreat, the inevitable happened. During a lively discussion about values, one of our children said, "Hey, Mom and Dad, we've been talking about all our family values for a few years now. So ... what are y'all's?"

Uh-oh.

I'm a bit embarrassed to say that, after all those years of discussing family values with our children, and after spending so much time watching them explore, adopt, and discard different potential values, John and I had never taken the time to write ours down. Without realizing it, we were having one of those parental "Do as I say, not as I do" moments. But, given the fact that we'd put them through a process of defining, preserving, and transferring their family values in their own homes, John and I knew it was well past time for us to "walk the talk." We spent the rest of that weekend articulating our values in front of our children.

At that point in our lives, identifying our values wasn't an aspirational exercise; rather, we simply looked back at the past thirty years and explored what had mattered most to us as we matured as husband and wife, raised our children, served as missionaries in Brazil, worked in executive leadership for a missions organization, and represented Chick-fil-A. When you're doing this at age twenty, it's more about what you *want* to do and how you *aspire* to act. But when you're doing it in your mid-fifties, like we were, it is more about what *have* you done and how *did* you act? It wasn't about planning; it was about looking back over our family's long history and engaging in a process of self-discovery, using the evidence of the past to lay out who we were and what we believed as a couple and as a family.

Our first two values, faith and family, were obvious. John and I were both raised in loving Christian homes with parents who stayed together, so we were blessed with wonderful examples of strong, godly marriages. And of course, the love of Christ was shared openly in the homes we grew up in and in the home we built for our children. We had traveled the world as a family to share the good news of Jesus, so faith had definitely been a bedrock value for the White family over the decades. As we reflected on the decisions we'd made, the causes we supported, the discussions we'd had, the challenges we'd overcome, and more, our other three values fell into place pretty easily: integrity, generosity, and gratitude. Of course, we haven't been perfect models of these five values every time, but we can say with confidence these are the five areas where we have strived as a couple and a family to invest our time, energy, and resources.

Standing on Values in Times of Adversity

As edifying as it was to look back on the life we'd lived up to that point and to identify the guiding principles we'd followed as a family, I must admit several decisions in our adult life would have been much easier if we'd already had these five values hanging on our kitchen wall. Fortunately, that *was* the case for our children. In fact, to be fully transparent, our family was going through a difficult season leading up to that 2011 family assembly when Maurice led our children through the values exercises. One of our four children was in the process of making some personal decisions that would have been in stark conflict with the values we had raised them with. At that point, we hadn't written our values down, but all six of us had a general understanding of what it meant to be a member of the White family, including what was inbounds *and* what was out-of-bounds. With one of our adult children on the verge of making what the rest of us knew was a terrible decision, John and I realized we were late in identifying and formalizing the values of our family. Moreover, we knew we had to encourage our children to grow beyond *our* family values and take ownership of their own.

As we continued to discuss personal and family values over the next few years, this one adult child continued to ride the line between who and what they were *tempted* to be and who and what they knew God had *made* them to be. It was those many discussions about values that tipped the scales to the side of faithfulness. After years of struggle and personal conflict, our child came to terms with the fact that God had made them and called them for more than what they were tempted to do, and they closed the door to that area of temptation for good. As a parent, we could not have been prouder. And, as a proponent of defining specific family and personal values, the message could not have been clearer: our values show us and the world who we are, and that is never more important than when we feel pulled to do or become something we are not. If it weren't for all the time our family had spent talking about and praying over what was important to us—truly, deeply important to us individually and as a family—this story might not have had a happy ending. Praise God, His timing for these discussions was perfect!

A crisis creates a sense of urgency in articulating values. In times of adversity, sickness, brokenness, and indecision, you realize that if you had set your values in stone earlier, you would now have them to fall back on. Conversely, not having them when you need them leaves you without boundaries and direction, which can only make a difficult time worse. In our situation, it would have been a lot easier if we had already clearly articulated and communicated our family values. Then we could have simply pulled them out and used that as a reference point in the family discussion about the decision our child was trying to make. Even though we had raised our children in an atmosphere of faith, family, integrity, generosity, and gratitude, we didn't have the firm guardrails of clearly stated values in place when we needed them most.

It's best to have your values set before you get into a crisis. The heat of the moment is not the best time to make important decisions about who you are, what you want, and how you want to live. The goal should be to work these things out for your family early so they're in place in the moment of tough decisions. Teaching your children early establishes a firm foundation of godly principles that will shape their upbringing and moral character well into adulthood. If you don't have something concrete to serve as a mental and emotional anchor, your emotions are going to carry you down a road you don't want to go. Your values must be decided apart from that, away from the urgency and anxiety of a crisis. Then, they're already in place and ready to inform you and hopefully guide you in your decisions. If you wait until the heat of the moment to try to set the guardrails for your life, you'll end up setting those barriers far away from where you'd otherwise know they should go. Don't leave your children, regardless of their age, to figure this out alone when the world is pressing in on them. Take the initiative to help them define and *own* their values before they ever get to that point.

Two Benefits of Clarifying Values

Getting clear on what we, as a family, value has provided a world of benefits to us as we work, play, engage one another, and interact with our children, grandchildren, and others. But I've also been surprised at how big an impact clear values have had on me individually—especially when it comes to deciding what I should and should not be doing. Having clearly stated values alongside my personal purpose statement (to glorify God by investing in relationships, influencing culture, and inspiring godly character) has given me the clarity to identify and focus only on the specific tasks I believe God has set before me. It's enabled me to become much more comfortable in my own skin, to be who I truly am, and to do the things God has specifically equipped me to do.

I'm the only one who can be a wife to John. I'm the only one who can be a mother to my children. I'm the only one who can be my grandchildren's Mimi. I'm the only one who is Truett and Jeannette Cathy's daughter. Being clear on my purpose has helped me to just be ... *me* and to use all the talents, skills, personality, and opportunities God's given me to have an influence on the world. It's clarified the arenas God has called me to operate in. If I have the chance to invest myself into something related to faith, family, integrity, generosity, or gratitude, I'm going to seriously consider that opportunity.

Likewise, if I have the chance to invest myself into something that is *not* in one of those key areas, I feel much more personal freedom and "permission" to say no. I used to feel horrible saying no to things. I didn't want to disappoint people, and I didn't want to accidentally miss out on a big blessing God had in store for me by saying no to opportunities—even if it was something I wasn't particularly excited about doing. When you aren't clear on your highest-priority values, you always feel a hint of fear that you'll miss out on some amazing blessing if you say no to *anything*. Frankly, that's exhausting. That's why I love the freedom I get in the boundaries that come with defining your values. It enables me to say no.

No, I cannot do *this* because God's called me to focus my energy in other areas. For me, those other areas include things like writing and reading books about faith and family, serving in our local church, spending my days working with our nonprofit ministries of Lifeshape and Impact 360 Institute, and giving support and appreciation to our Support Center staff at Chick-fil-A and our many incredible Operators and Team Members. These things are life-giving to me because they sit squarely within my values of faith, family, integrity, generosity, and gratitude. I have more than enough of these opportunities to fill my schedule, so I don't have to feel guilty about not doing something that doesn't fit into one of these categories.

HOW TO DEFINE YOUR VALUES

Our friend and mentor Maurice Graham helped us and our children narrow down our specific family values over the course of several long, insightful conversations. Since then, John and I have found a wonderful tool that has helped make this process easier, especially as we now walk our grandchildren through this exercise every year. We use two tools—a *word bank* and *values cards*. Our family started with the word bank and had great success, but we've moved on to the values cards now that we're regularly teaching values lessons to our grandchildren. Both processes are similar, and I'll provide both resources for you in this chapter using the wonderful *Personal Values Card Sort* tool developed by W. R. Miller, J. C'de Baca, D. B. Matthews, and P. L. Wilbourne of the University of New Mexico. The word bank provided within this chapter comes from the researchers' cards, and the full set of cards—which you can copy and cut for personal use—is provided in the appendix of this book.

How do you use these tools? It's actually a simple process... but don't mistake that to mean it's *easy*. It's definitely a challenge! In this chapter I'll focus on using the values cards that are included in this chapter, but you can just as easily use the word bank. After explaining the values card option, I'll give you some simple adjustments if you prefer not to photocopy and cut out your own set of cards.

Picture a deck of cards, but instead of numbers and suits, each card has a one-word value and its definition. Examples might be *gratitude, humility, honesty, integrity, faith, family, discipline, achievement, acceptance, structure, leadership, respect, safety,* and so on. There are dozens of potential values represented on the cards—a wide variety of areas that could be of particular importance to your family. Feel free to buy an actual deck of values cards (there are several options available online), or simply photocopy the values card template in the appendix of this book and cut the cards out yourself.

Now, let's walk through how you can use the values cards yourself and with your children. When we held our family assembly meeting in 2011, Maurice introduced the concept of personal and family values to our adult children. He started by challenging them with three probing questions:

1. What really matters to you?
2. What values govern how you live?
3. What values do you want others to recognize in you?

These are the same questions we ask when leading someone through this exercise. The discussions you can have around just these three questions can be life changing, especially as a precursor to the values cards exercise.

Once you have articulated what really matters to you and the general values you strive to live by, it's time to pull out the deck of values cards. Go through the deck one card at a time, seriously considering each value you see. You'll need to file the cards into three stacks:

1. This value is very important to me.
2. This value is (sort of) important to me.
3. This value is not important to me.

This will be harder than you might think, because every card represents something good and noble. No one wants to draw the integrity card, for example, and say, "Oh, integrity is not that important to me." But this exercise requires absolute honesty and self-examination. The deck of values cards might have fifty or more options. No one can live up to prioritizing fifty different core values!

While you should be mindful about thoughtfully reviewing the values, I encourage you not to think too much about each one. It's easy to get stuck trying to decide how important each value is to you—especially if you're prone to overthinking things. It may be hard, but try to trust your gut with this first pass through the deck. If you see a card and aren't immediately drawn to it, it probably doesn't belong in your "very important" pile, no matter how good and noble the value is. Trust me, this doesn't make you a bad person! The goal here isn't to prove how great you are; the goal is to identify the values that *most represent* what's truly important to you. If you can't be honest with yourself in whittling down the list of options, the whole exercise will be thrown off-kilter.

Once you make your three stacks—which could take a surprisingly long time—it's time to do the exact same thing again. But this time, you're only going to use the cards in your "really important" pile. That's right: the "sort of important" and "not that important" cards are done. Move them to the side. We don't need them anymore. All we care about now are the values you've identified as really important to you. Using only that stack of cards, go back through each one and divide them into three piles:

1. This value is very important to me.
2. This value is (sort of) important to me.
3. This value is not important to me.

I know it will be more difficult this time, and that's okay. Be as ruthless as you need to be with yourself, but you've got to move *some* of those values into a new "sort of important" and "not that important" pile.

At this point, if you have more than five cards in your "very important" pile, you'll need to repeat this elimination process one more time. No individual or family can be expected to live up to more than five key values, so you should keep going until you identify no more than five values you consider "really important" to you.

When Maurice led our children through a similar process, they groaned every time he made them refine their list of values a bit more. But, when we finished, our children were able to say with confidence, "*This* is what is important to me, and this is the kind of family we want to have for ourselves." It was a grueling process, but as we all discussed each one of their values, it was clear that our children had picked the perfect values for themselves. What they identified resonated perfectly with the wonderful, unique, godly man or woman the rest of us knew them to be. I pray you have the same experience when you do the exercise for yourself!

The Word Bank Option

If you choose to use the word bank below rather than the full set of cards, the process is almost exactly like what I outlined above. However, you'll be referring to a list of values rather than sorting through cards. Use the process above plus these three additional tips:

1. Look through the list of values. Write your *top ten* on a piece of paper. If you feel strongly about a value that is *not* represented on the word bank, add it to your list. The *Personal Values Card Sort* is a wonderful tool, but don't be surprised if you recognize a value in yourself that isn't represented on the list.

2. If you are married, you and your spouse should *each* do Step 1 separately, meaning you will have one list of ten values and your spouse will have their list of ten values for a total of twenty. Come back together and discuss the "why" behind choosing each value to make sure you each understand why each value is important to the other.

3. Now, start whittling down your list of ten values (or twenty, if married) using the same process outlined above, separating them into the three categories:
   1. This value is very important to me.
   2. This value is (sort of) important to me.
   3. This value is not important to me.
4. Keep refining the list until you arrive at a final list of three to five family values.

Personal Values Word Bank[1]

Acceptance: to be accepted as I am	Accuracy: to be accurate in my opinions and beliefs
Achievement: to have important accomplishments	Adventure: to have new and exciting experiences
Attractiveness: to be physically attractive	Authority: to be in charge of and responsible for others
Autonomy: to be self-determined and independent	Beauty: to appreciate beauty around me
Caring: to take care of others	Challenge: to take on difficult tasks and problems
Change: to have a life full of change and variety	Comfort: to have a pleasant and comfortable life
Commitment: to make enduring, meaningful commitments	Compassion: to feel and act on concern for others
Contribution: to make a lasting contribution in the world	Cooperation: to work collaboratively with others

Courtesy: to be considerate and polite toward others	Creativity: to have new and original ideas
Dependability: to be reliable and trustworthy	Duty: to carry out my duties and obligations
Ecology: to live in harmony with the environment	Excitement: to have a life full of thrills and stimulation
Faithfulness: to be loyal and true in relationships	Fame: to be known and recognized
Family: to have a happy, loving family	Fitness: to be physically fit and strong
Flexibility: to adjust to new circumstances easily	Forgiveness: to be forgiving of others
Friendship: to have close, supportive friends	Fun: to play and have fun
Generosity: to give what I have to others	Genuineness: to act in a manner that is true to who I am
God's Will: to seek and obey the will of God	Growth: to keep changing and growing
Health: to be physically well and healthy	Helpfulness: to be helpful to others
Honesty: to be honest and truthful	Hope: to maintain a positive and optimistic outlook
Humility: to be modest and unassuming	Humor: to see the humorous side of myself and the world
Independence: to be free from dependence on others	Industry: to work hard and well at my life tasks
Inner Peace: to experience personal peace	Intimacy: to share my innermost experiences with others
Justice: to promote fair and equal treatment for all	Knowledge: to learn and contribute valuable knowledge

Leisure: to take time to relax and enjoy	Loved: to be loved by those close to me
Loving: to give love to others	Mastery: to be competent in my everyday activities
Mindfulness: to live conscious and mindful of the present moment	Moderation: to avoid excesses and find a middle ground
Monogamy: to have one close, loving relationship	Nonconformity: to question and challenge authority and norms
Nurturance: to take care of and nurture others	Openness: to be open to new experiences, ideas, and options
Order: to have a life that is well ordered and organized	Passion: to have deep feelings about ideas, activities, or people
Pleasure: to feel good	Popularity: to be well liked by many people
Power: to have control over others	Purpose: to have meaning and direction in my life
Rationality: to be guided by reason and logic	Realism: to see and act realistically and practically
Responsibility: to make and carry out responsible decisions	Risk: to take risks and chances
Romance: to have intense, exciting love in my life	Safety: to be safe and secure
Self-Acceptance: to accept myself as I am	Self-Control: to be disciplined in my own actions
Self-Esteem: to feel good about myself	Self-Knowledge: to have a deep and honest understanding of myself
Service: to be of service to others	Sexuality: to have an active and satisfying sex life
Simplicity: to live life simply, with minimal needs	Solitude: to have time and space where I can be apart from others

Spirituality: to grow and mature spiritually	Stability: to have a life that stays fairly consistent
Tolerance: to accept and respect those who differ from me	Tradition: to follow respected patterns of the past
Virtue: to live a morally pure and excellent life	Wealth: to have plenty of money
World Peace: to work to promote peace in the world	

START TEACHING VALUES EARLY

Seeing how powerful it is to properly identify and target your family values makes me regret not being more intentional about doing this with our children when they were young. While we still practiced the values of faith, family, integrity, generosity, and gratitude back then, I can't help but wonder how much more effective and efficient we could have been in our family, business, and missionary life if we had been as laser-focused on these five areas then as we are now. I fully believe that you can change the future of the world by raising children with godly values, and I don't believe this has ever been more important than it is today.

I've lived through several major changes in our cultural and political life—the assassination of John F. Kennedy, the Civil Rights Movement, the Vietnam War, the passage of Roe v. Wade, the Cold War, the rise in single-parent families, the drug epidemic, and 9/11, just to name a few—but what I see going on in recent years is unlike anything I've ever seen before. We live in a fallen world, and this world will continue to break down in every way imaginable unless the people of God stand up and make a change. There has to be some intentionality in reversing the downward moral slide of modern culture. God didn't create us to live a life of deterioration; He created us for a life of abundance! But that abundant life must be built on a foundation, and far too many families aren't taking that foundational approach seriously. I believe focusing on family values—*your* family's values—is a great place to start turning the tide.

Of course, John and I can't go back in time and change the focus we put on this with our own children when they were young . . . but it's something we're now doing with our grandchildren. When our first grandchild, Ashlynn, turned thirteen years old, we started an annual tradition we call the Assembly for Grands, a special gathering we hold every year with our grandchildren ages thirteen and up, which I will explain more fully later. That first year, it was just Ashlynn; as of 2022, six of our grandchildren now participate in this gathering, and others will be added when they turn thirteen. As part of this yearly event, John and I lead them through the values cards exercise. We are careful not to give the impression that the values they select will be the same five values they'll *always* prioritize. Our values change and mature as *we* change and mature—and that's especially true with children. We don't want any of our "grands" to feel unduly locked in to a value they selected at thirteen if it simply doesn't fit at eighteen. There is a huge maturity gap between a thirteen-year-old and an eighteen-year-old, after all. It's a much bigger gap than what exists between a thirty- and a forty-year-old. So, we walk the children through this exercise from scratch every year.

We record and track the values they select each year, but we do not assume that's where they'll start the following year. Instead, every year we have each child start with the full deck of values cards and whittle them down anew. Generally, several of the same values are chosen, but it's common for one or two to change year over year. Tracking all of this enables us to see patterns emerge and be able to identify which values are consistent and which ones are more fluid.

We also have to be cautious not to influence the teens as they select their value cards. Children often feel like they need to choose *the best* values or the ones that are most important to their parents or grandparents. We don't want them to pick the values they *wish* they had. We want each grandchild to pick only the values that truly reflect who they are and what they hold dear. We're trying to teach them to be true to the wonderful, unique young men and women God made them to be and to strive to reach their full potential in those key areas. It's not about pleasing Mom, Dad, Mimi, or Papa; it's about pleasing their heavenly Father by recognizing and rejoicing in the passions and interests He's placed in their hearts.

THE WRITING'S ON THE WALL

In the next five chapters, I will pull back a bit and explore what each of my family's five core values means to us. I will talk about how we chose each one and, more importantly, how we *live out* each one. But take note: I'll do this only as an example to you of what's possible when you get clarity on your values. Faith, family, integrity, generosity, and gratitude are *our* family values; they almost certainly will not be yours. Sure, we may share one or two in common, but every family needs to identify their *specific mix of values* for themselves. That's why the value cards exercise is so important.

I encourage you to spend time over the next few days or weeks exploring what your family values might be. You can do this the same way we do, using the resources in this book or buying your own deck of value cards. Then, once you've identified the top three to five values that stand out to your family, get together with your children and grandchildren to explain what your family values are and why you selected those specific five. Talk about how you have lived these values out in the past and how you'll continue to do so in the future.

I also challenge you to post these values around your home in some way. We have our values prominently posted around the sitting room off of our kitchen. As you look overhead, you'll see five wooden signs hung high and surrounding you, with one word painted on each to represent our five values. Our children have done something similar in their homes. It reminds me of the Lord's command in Deuteronomy after He gave Moses the Ten Commandments:

Keep these words in your heart that I am telling you today. Do your best to teach them to your children. Talk about them when you sit in your house and when you walk on the road and when you lie down and when you get up. Tie them as something special to see on your hand and on your forehead. *Write them beside the door of your house and on your gates.* (Deuteronomy 6:6–9, NLV, emphasis added)

There's just something powerful about writing these things down and posting them for all to see.

Growing up, my mother kept a small sign in our kitchen that read, "Only one life 'twill soon be passed. Only what's done for Christ will last." [2] It's a line from a poem written by a late-nineteenth/early-twentieth-century missionary named Charles Studd. From my early childhood to today, years after my parents have passed away, I don't remember ever being in that kitchen without seeing that sign. It's a part of me. That saying, "Only what's done for Christ will last," has been ringing in my ears my whole life. In the same way, all my grandchildren are growing up in homes that have their family values proudly posted on the wall. They'll walk past them a hundred times a day, *every day*, from the day they're born to the day they leave home. That kind of intentional exposure leaves a mark on a young person's heart and mind. It plants that seed deep, burying the family values in the core of their being. They may not realize it now, as children, but that seed will bear much fruit throughout their lives. That's the power of writing these values down and keeping them in front of you (and your children) every day.

CHAPTER 3

OUR FAMILY VALUES #1:
FAITH

"**H**ave a seat!"
How many times has a host welcomed you into their kitchen, dining room, or living room with that greeting? We hear it all the time. And what do we do? We sit down, of course! We don't think twice about stepping in front of a chair and dropping all our weight onto a seat we've never sat in before. How do we know

the chair will support us? How do we know we won't fall right through it, crashing our tailbone onto the hard, unforgiving floor beneath?

Faith.

It might sound silly, but this is the example I often use when explaining the concept of faith to a child. When we see a chair, we assume it can hold us up. We don't check it out at all. We don't check the legs to see if they are loose. We simply trust as we fall into a chair, assuming it was designed to hold us and that it will do just that. To me, that is a simple way to illustrate the idea of putting your trust—your *faith*—in something. In the same way, when I put my faith in God as a young girl, I didn't know all the ins and outs about Him. I just knew the basics, and I had to believe He would support me when I put my complete trust in Him alone.

In this chapter, I want to begin our exploration into my family's five core values—faith, family, integrity, generosity, and gratitude—by focusing specifically on the value of faith. As I explained in the previous chapter, I don't expect every reader to name faith among their five key values (everyone's list will be different), but I do want to use my family's five values as an example. My hope is to show you why we chose our specific values, how they play out in our lives, and how we've tried to pass them along to our children. In doing so, I want to help you articulate the same for the values you've selected. We need to start, of course, by understanding what the value means in principle before we see it in practice.

So . . . what do I mean by *faith*?

WHAT IS FAITH?

That is such a big question—one that is far beyond the scope of this book. Philosophers and theologians have debated for thousands of years about what faith is and where it comes from. There is little chance that I, the daughter of a chicken cook from Georgia, could add much to such a grand discussion that has been going on for millennia. Instead of trying to reinvent the wheel, I want to keep things simple by focusing on the two definitions of faith that have meant the most to me—one from Scripture and one from a dear friend and ministry partner.

The author of the book of Hebrews provides what many believe to be *the* definition of biblical faith: "Faith shows the reality of what we hope for; it is the evidence of things we cannot see" (Hebrews 11:1, NLT). I like that: *the evidence of things we cannot see.* It's like the chair illustration above, in that we are sure the chair beneath us will support us when we fall into it. It could also be something as mundane as trusting that your spouse will pick you up from the airport like they said they would. After all, you aren't in the car with them. You've told them what time to arrive and trusted them when they said they would be there. Using the Bible's terminology, you cannot *see* them, but you can still be sure they'll be there. If we weren't sure, we would have backup plans, wouldn't we? We would have our spouse's assurance *and* we would have a rental car reservation *and* we would most likely have the Uber app open and ready to order a ride home. But we don't do that, do we? No, we trust what our spouse tells us. We have *faith* in them. And we step out of the airport fully expecting to see them drive up, ready to take us home.

Of course, if your spouse has a long history of breaking promises, you may have a weaker faith. If your spouse has a long track record of showing up for you in the face of any obstacle, you'll have a stronger faith. Either way, it's still faith that you're demonstrating. And that personal experience with the object of your faith brings me to my second-favorite definition of faith. Jonathan Morrow, our colleague at the Impact 360 Institute gap year program, defines faith as *active trust in what you have good reason to believe is true*. I love this understanding of faith! It's *active trust* in that faith calls you to *do* something, but it's not *blind* faith. Rather, it's trusting in something that has *proven itself to be true*. Again, if your spouse has shown over and over that they'll move heaven and earth to keep their word to you, you have every reason to put your *active trust* in them to pick you up at the airport. They've given you no reason to doubt, just like a chair has given you no reason to suspect it will collapse beneath you. This kind of faith is not blind, and it is not based on how you may *feel* at any given moment. It is reasonable. It's based on the truth you have good reason to believe.

We can have that same certainty when it comes to our faith in God. We don't have to simply "trust and believe" with no evidence whatsoever of God's presence. No, we can point to the Lord's long history of intervention in our lives and in the lives of others. We can examine the miracles He's brought about, the comfort He's provided, and the devotion of those who have put their faith in Him. We can look at the beauty of a sunset or the intricacies of a DNA molecule and trust that there is a master painter and architect behind it. We can point to history, archaeology, science, and other sources of information. We do not have to be afraid of empirical evidence—we should use it!

So often, we try to overcomplicate the concept of faith. We surround it in a million *what ifs* and allow our suspicious minds to carry us off into a land of confusion. But faith is so, so simple—so simple even a child can understand it. In the Gospel of Matthew, Jesus says, "Let the children come to me. Don't stop them! For the Kingdom of Heaven belongs to those who are like these children" (Matthew 19:14, NLT). Did you catch that? Jesus says that heaven is made up not of scholars, scientists, and theologians (although they certainly have their place). Rather, heaven is made up of those with a childlike wonder, those who are able to place their full faith and confidence in something, as the book of Hebrews describes, that they cannot see. My friend Jonathan Morrow would say they are able to do that because God has proven Himself to them already; He's given them every reason to trust He is there.

I placed my faith in Jesus when I was a child of seven years old. I knew He loved me and cared for me. I knew He said that if I would believe, I would receive eternal life. It was such a simple decision that I made as a young girl, and yet it has made all the difference in who I have been throughout my life, who I am today in my sixties, and who I will be throughout eternity.

MY BACKGROUND OF FAITH

My parents were both believers who took us to church every Sunday. They recognized that worshipping the Lord with other believers was important, so church was a priority for our family growing up. It wasn't always easy or convenient, but it was something my parents were very intentional about. My parents gave me my first understanding of a God who loved me, loving each other and their children so well, diligently taking us to church, leading Bible study classes, and studying the Bible on their own—my mom at the kitchen table and my dad in the study. Their influence cannot be overstated when it came to planting that seed of faith in me and my brothers.

In my early years, we always had a lot of revivals happening at our church. For us, a revival was a weeklong event with speakers and activity at the church every night. This was the early 1960s, and the Christian music of the day seemed to put a lot of focus on being ready for Jesus's return. That message seeped into my brain, and I became concerned with being ready when Jesus came back. I was only seven at the time, but the matter of my eternal salvation weighed heavily on my mind. After one particularly compelling revival service, I came home and talked to my parents about it. I said, "I know that you love me, and the Bible says that God loves me. But what does that really mean for me?"

For some reason, they felt like I needed to talk to the pastor, so they invited our local pastor, Brother Brown, to come by our house one afternoon after school. I remember being very excited about the fact that our pastor was coming to our house to talk to me. I thought that was a *really* big deal. My father even came home from work early, which was honestly an even bigger deal! It was just my mom and dad, our pastor, and me sitting in our living room. As the youngest child always competing for attention against my two brothers, I enjoyed getting such special, individual attention that day.

Brother Brown took out his Bible to read John 3:16 and unpacked it a little bit, and I prayed to give my life to Jesus, to follow Him and to be obedient to Him (whatever that looked like in my childish mind at the time). My brothers—one and two years older than me—were sent outside to play during this meeting, and they told me later that they were discussing me and the pastor while they were out there, wondering what we were talking about and if it was something they needed to do. Not long after that, they both talked to my parents about choosing to follow Jesus, and all three of us were baptized together at our local church, Lovejoy Baptist. I always thought it was significant that I made that decision on my own. There weren't many things I got to do first being the youngest of three, but this time I wasn't following something my brothers had already done. I felt a sense of pride and ownership in my decision to follow Jesus. Even at that young age, I didn't feel like it was my parents' faith or my older brothers' faith. It was mine.

Accepting Christ at such a young age was a blessing, because I believe my active faith protected me as a teenager. I was put into a lot of situations with many different young people—friends who *were not* Christians—that could have gone a very different direction if I weren't already filtering my decisions through my faith. It is a testament to God's faithfulness that He protected me from those mistakes that have taken so many young lives off track. In fact, looking back over my life, I believe every big decision I've ever made from age seven on has gone through the filter of my faith in Christ. It has been *the* key factor in my marriage, parenting, career, ministry, relationships, finances, giving, time management, and every other area of my life.

Someone recently shared that she was asked to give a short presentation to a group of Christians about how she integrates her faith into her work, which is a common topic among groups of Christian professionals. For John and me, though, faith is not something we've "integrated" into our lives. It is the bedrock on which everything in our lives is built. I don't integrate my faith into my work; I've built my career on the foundation of my faith. I don't integrate my faith into my family life; I've built my marriage and our family on that foundation. Faith is absolutely foundational to every part of our lives, whether it's work, family, friends, fun, how we spend our time, how we give our time and money, or anything else. Everything we have, everything we do, and everything we are has sprung from that fertile ground of faith.

BRAVER AND BETTER: OUR FAITH IN ACTION

Over the course of my life, I can honestly say that my faith has made me *braver* and *better*. John and I have faced situations and decisions throughout our marriage that have seemed insurmountable. There were so many times I saw what God was calling us to do, and my main thought was, *How in the world are we going to do this, Lord?* But then, right when I needed it, I felt a wave of courage wash over me—courage that could only have come from the Lord. His bravery has made me stronger in the face of seemingly impossible decisions.

People may look at our life now and think we haven't a care in the world, and it's true that God has been abundantly good to our family and has showered us with His blessings. But that doesn't mean I've never had to worry about things like money, relationships, ministry issues, and whether my children would make the right decisions as they faced battles of their own. There are crises we all face at times, and our family is no different. However, God has shown me time and again that difficult times can and should be opportunities for tremendous growth—if we approach them through the lens of faith. That's the time I grow most: when I am in a challenging situation or facing a critical decision. It's when I lean in most to my faith and dependency on the God who made me and who I can trust to guide me.

Likewise, I know my faith has made me better by giving me direction in the decisions I've made since I was seven years old. God has been my compass and my guide through the journeys of life, from the intense pressure of being one of the youngest Operators in Chick-fil-A's history, to the fear of diving into the unknown culture of Brazil as a missionary, to trying to figure out my role in the world and in the kingdom once we returned home to the States. At every point, I've tried to rely on God's Word as "a lamp to guide my feet and a light for my path" (Psalm 119:105, NLT).

Of course, maintaining that lens of faith can be difficult when life gets hard, when the waves of adversity are crashing against you, and it takes every bit of strength you can muster to simply hold on and not be swept away in the current. I've experienced so many of these times myself, difficulties and decisions that could have left me discouraged or even depressed if it had not been for my faith that God was with me and that I could trust Him to see me through the darkness. I believe that is what David meant in Psalm 23, when he wrote, "Even when I walk through the darkest valley, I will not be afraid, for you are close beside me. Your rod and your staff protect and comfort me" (Psalm 23:4, NLT). Or when the prophet Isaiah wrote,

> People of Zion, who live in Jerusalem, you will weep no more. How gracious he will be when you cry for help! As soon as he hears, he will answer you. Although the Lord gives you the bread of adversity and the water of affliction, your teachers will be hidden no more; with your own eyes you will see them. Whether you turn to the right or to the left, your ears will hear a voice behind you, saying, "This is the way; walk in it." (Isaiah 30:19–21, NIV)

I have felt Him close beside me. I have heard His voice saying, "This is the way." Whether things are going well or going poorly, the fact that I have placed my faith in the God who created me and the fact that I am a follower of Jesus Christ gives me a tremendous amount of peace and comfort in difficult times. I honestly do not know how people get through the most challenging times of life without Him. I know I never could.

Now, that doesn't mean I haven't scratched my head a time or two and wondered what on earth God was thinking! In fact, I've been pretty bold with Him on several occasions, asking *why* He would lead us to do something so far outside our normal experience. Sometimes He's answered, and sometimes it's taken a while to see His plan come to fruition—but I don't think He's ever minded me asking Him *why*. That's what children do, right? We ask our parents why *this* and why *that*. I recently asked my son John what he wished I had done differently as his mother when he was young. He said, "The one thing I wish you would have done more when we were little was to tell us the *why* behind some of the things you wanted us to do. That would have helped me understand your reasoning, which would have made it easier to go along with it." Fair enough, because I do the same thing with my heavenly Father!

When we know *why* He wants us to do something, it makes it so much easier to do it. And yet He often doesn't show us His reasons—at least not immediately. Instead, He calls us to simply start a new adventure, trusting Him in faith to show up in His time. That's the crux of the issue, isn't it? To actually start moving when He says move, even if He hasn't told us *where to go?* That's what we see in the Bible with God's call to Abraham (then known as Abram) in Genesis 12: "The LORD had said to Abram, 'Go from your country, your people and your father's household *to the land I will show you*'" (Genesis 12:1, NIV, emphasis added).

John and I have had a "go to the land I will show you" calling twice in our lives. The first was when God called us into the mission field. That call caught me completely by surprise. We were in our mid-twenties, newly married, and John was in law school. My life plan was crystal clear in my mind: get John through law school, move back to Atlanta with my family, and stay home with our children while John enjoyed a successful career with my father and brothers at Chick-fil-A. That was my dream, and it was a *happy* dream. I couldn't wait to live that life. So, when John first told me God had put a burden for international missions on his heart, I shut him down completely. It wasn't even a possibility to me. It took a few years for God to soften my heart and open my mind to the very idea, but even then, we didn't know *where* He was leading us. In retrospect, I can see that God knew from the start that He wanted us serving in Brazil, but at the time, all we knew was that He was calling us to *go*. Once we took the first few steps, He showed us the next few, then the next . . . all the way to Brazil.

The second Abram-like calling was twenty years later. After serving for ten years in South America, John was asked to return to the States and serve in an executive role with the International Mission Board (IMB), the mission agency that had sent us to Brazil. Though this was a surprise, at least we knew where we were going (Richmond, Virginia) and what he'd be doing. When God started calling us away from Richmond several years later, though, things were much less clear. Although John enjoyed his job and had helped write his own "dream" job description, he had a growing sense of discontentment with his work. Despite sending and supporting missionaries all over the world, he felt unfulfilled, as though he were no longer doing the work God wanted him to do. After months of prayer and introspection, we heard God clearly telling us to leave Richmond and the IMB. The problem was, that's where the calling stopped. There was no *why*. There was no *where* or *what now*. God told us to move ... and then He went silent for months.

This was the most trying time in my life of faith—even more so than when we had first been called to missionary service. At least then, we knew what we would be doing. Now in our late forties, we had a small amount of savings, children in college, and no idea what we were supposed to do. We only knew we had to be obedient ... and so, we were. John resigned his position, we moved back to Atlanta, and we spent several days with Tom Patterson in his home, where Tom facilitated a LifePlan experience to help us discover and identify the next step in God's plan for our lives. Fortunately, as I've written about in my other books, God made His plan known and has led us into an incredible "second act" in our fifties and sixties, full of blessings we might have missed if we had not held fast to our family value of faith.

We've learned through experience that God does not mind us asking *why*, and it does not betray a weak faith. The problem is when you refuse to be obedient *until* or *unless* God reveals His full plan. You cannot hold the will of God hostage by your unwillingness to go when He tells you to go; you'll only miss the blessings He has in store for you further down the road. Like my friend Jonathan Morrow says, faith is *active trust in what we have reason to believe is true.* Active trust is just that: *active.* It is a faith that moves us away from Point A—even if God hasn't fully revealed what or where Point B is.

TEACHING FAITH TO THE NEXT GENERATION

As parents, we wanted to live up to the calling of 2 Corinthians 2:15: "Our lives are a Christ-like fragrance rising up to God" (NLT). We wanted to be that *fragrance* of Christ for our children. No parent is perfect, of course, and John and I were certainly no exception. However, we did have an intentional agenda to make Christ attractive to our children through our actions. We structured discussions and activities around getting their hearts and minds engaged, leading them to recognize their individual need for a personal relationship with Jesus. Faith had been our most important, lifelong value, and we wanted to pass that value on to our children.

The Bible celebrates having children in our lives, whether they're our children, grandchildren, or extended family members. The psalmist declared, "Children are a gift from the LORD; they are a reward from him. Children born to a young man are like arrows in a warrior's hands. How joyful is the man whose quiver is full of them!" (Psalm 127:3–5, NLT). And of grandchildren, Proverbs says, "Grandchildren are the crowning glory of the aged" (Proverbs 17:6, NLT). How true that is! John and I have been blessed with sixteen precious grandchildren, and each one is a crown on our graying heads!

Since our children are such a precious gift from God, our goal has always been to honor Him by returning them to Him—that is, doing everything we can to make sure they grow closer in their walk with Him and raise their own children to do the same. We wanted to raise children to walk in a manner worthy of the calling God had placed on their lives, to respect Him, to live according to His wisdom, and to maintain a kingdom-first perspective of eternity. While we have always had a close family bond—a value we'll discuss in the following chapter—we wanted our children (and now our grandchildren) to understand that they were children of their heavenly Father *first* and children of their earthly parents *second*. The best way we knew to do that was to make sure we were modeling what that looks like with our own lives. We know that our very existence is based on glorifying the God who created us. As Isaiah wrote, "Bring all who claim me as their God, for I have made them for my glory. It was I who created them" (Isaiah 43:7, NLT). If we weren't living with that mindset, we knew there was little chance our children ever would. Their life of faith, in so many ways, depended on *our* life of faith—and we were determined not to let them down.

When it comes to teaching children anything, especially about what it means to walk with the Lord, we believe more is caught than taught. That is, children will generally do *what they see their parents doing*, not what their parents *tell them to do*. From early childhood, our concept of who God is and how He loves us starts with what we see in our parents—how they love each other, how they love their children, and how they love their God.

Because our children mostly grew up in Brazil, working in the mission field with us, they were able to see our faith in action all day, every day. They got to see us living with complete trust in God for His provision and protection all through those years. We couldn't rely on the comforts and conveniences that we ourselves had grown up with or that the rest of our family in the States was relying on at the time. We had a very modest lifestyle during those years, but we were wealthy in faith. Our children got to learn that that was enough.

Prayer is obviously a key component to the life of faith, and teaching our children how to talk and listen to God is an important job for us as parents. This does not mean that every family has to adhere to a strict, structured routine of nightly prayers as a family or a scheduled daily group devotional. Sure, those things can be wonderful tools in raising children of faith, but not every family is wired for that kind of structure. We certainly weren't. We went to church regularly and prayed together at meals and as needs arose, but we were not a family that had a set, all-hands-on-deck, daily devotional time. I think it's great if that works for your family, but our children were always bouncing off the walls and doing all kinds of things we could rarely pull them away from. They did, however, grow up seeing their mother and father prioritize their *personal* walks with the Lord.

John and I have always had dedicated spots in our home where we study the Word, journal, and pray. Today, John has his chair in our den. That is holy ground for him. In fact, I've rearranged the furniture in that room several times, but I'm always careful not to move his chair. That's a special place where he meets with the Lord. Our children and grandchildren understand that if John is in that chair, he's spending time in the Word and talking to the Lord. I'm not quite as structured as that, but I do have a spot in our bedroom where I keep my Bible and journal. That's where I tend to get away for one-on-one time with God.

Seeing us engage in that kind of regular, consistent, dedicated, and personal time with God has made an impact on our children and now on our grandchildren. Again, more is caught than taught. We've tried to teach them how to live, but we've tried even harder to *show* them how to live—partly through our example and partly through intentional activities and experiences we've created throughout their lives. I recently asked my children about this, and they all confirmed what John and I always suspected: it was less about what we *said* and more about what we *did*. Experience is always the best teacher. We'll talk about several of these experiences later in the book.

LEAVING A LEGACY OF FAITH

In thinking about our faith as a family value, and particularly thinking about the ways in which John and I have tried to be intentional about passing that value on to our children and grandchildren, I can think of no better example than what we call "Papa's Bibles." My husband is a voracious reader of Scripture. He reads through the entire Bible at least once a year, reading from the Old Testament one day and the New Testament the next plus a psalm every day. As he reads, he makes notes in the margins of his Bible, calling out things that stand out to him, applications from sermons and lectures he's listened to, prayer needs, references to other books for further exploration on the passage he's reading, and so on. His mother taught him from a young age that the Bible is not only a book we should revere but one we should relentlessly study—and that means marking it up to kingdom come!

As our children were getting older and closer to marriage, John thought it would be a special family memento if he were to give each of our children one of his marked-up Bibles as a wedding gift. As our two daughters and two sons grew up and got married, that's exactly what he did. He proudly presented each one with a special Bible from their father, each uniquely filled with his thoughts, feelings, journaling, and insights on each page of God's Word. The children loved it, and John and I were warmed knowing these Bibles would be meaningful family heirlooms—legacy pieces—long after we're gone.

Fast forward a few years, and our family was suddenly growing by leaps and bounds with grandchildren. John had still maintained his daily Scripture reading, filling a Bible with new notes, prayers, and journal entries every year. He then had an ambitious thought: what if he gave each one of his grandchildren a personalized Bible, each one filled cover to cover with their grandfather's handwritten insights? He bought a big stack of Bibles, lined them up on a bookshelf, and got to work!

With so many grandchildren, this is at least a fifteen-year project. I'm amazed that he's taking this goal so seriously, although I really shouldn't be. His strong faith and his commitment to his family are two of the main reasons I fell in love with him in the first place!

We've been open with the "grands" about this ongoing project, and they are each excited to receive their special gift on their wedding day, just like their parents did. None of them have received theirs yet—our oldest grandchild is seventeen as of this writing—but John's about halfway through his goal at this point. When he finishes one, he puts it back in its box on his bookshelf, pulls the next one down, and starts it the next day. It's truly an inspiration to watch, and it is a testament to the priority the family value of faith has in his life. I'm just honored to be on this journey with him, and I'm so grateful for such a strong man of faith who leads his family with the most powerful teaching tools at his disposal—God's Word and his example.

CHAPTER 4

OUR FAMILY VALUES #2: FAMILY

Growing up, I had a little notebook that I used as a type of journal. I didn't write in it every day or even every week. Instead, it was a place for me to jot down big things that I wanted for my life and things I was concerned about. That list changed in many ways as I grew up, always reflecting who I was at each stage of life. One thing that never changed, though, was the item at the top of my prayer list: I wanted to get married and have a lot of children. Specifically, I wanted six children—including a set of twins. That dream never wavered, and it was in my prayers every night. I was quite persistent with the Lord about giving me the family of my dreams!

As I've said before, at that time there was a big emphasis in the church around Jesus's imminent return to earth. It seemed like everyone was talking about Jesus coming back. Nearly every Christian song I heard talked about the trumpet sounding and the heavens opening to reveal Jesus coming in the clouds. As a fairly new Christian, it was certainly exciting... but, as a young girl daydreaming about one day becoming a wife and mother, I must admit it was a bit disturbing. I love Jesus more than anything, but I couldn't stand the thought of not having this family that I had always dreamed of. I remember so many nights when I'd go to bed praying, "God, I know You are coming back soon, and I can't wait to see You face to face. But... maybe You could wait just a little longer so I have a chance to grow up, get married, and have children?"

Well, fortunately for me, and despite the excitement about Jesus's "imminent" return in the 1960s, God decided to hold out at least long enough for my family dreams to come true. I met John at age nineteen, married him at twenty-one, and we had four wonderful children over the next seven years. A difficult delivery with my fourth—including a critical ambulance ride straight up a Brazilian mountainside to a private clinic with a specialized NICU (Neonatal Intensive Care Unit)—brought a sudden end to my childbearing years, so we never made it all the way to the six children I'd always expected, and I never got my twins. While we were in Brazil, I used to joke with John that if someone ever knocked on our door and left two babies sitting in a basket on our doorstep, we were keeping them. If twins showed up on my doorstep tomorrow, I still might!

Coming from a loving family myself, I have always had a passion for marriage and parenting. And it wasn't just that I wanted the *titles* of wife and mother; I was excited to accept the challenge of *becoming* a godly wife and mother. I wanted to partner with a godly man in life and ministry. I wanted to build a home and a family that could make an impact in the world for God's kingdom. I wanted to raise children to know God and teach them biblical principles in practical ways. In fact, my greatest desire was to watch my own children grow up and live as obedient followers of Jesus.

It's no wonder, then, that John and I identified *family* as one of our foundational family values. I don't think it's an exaggeration to say that everything we do, while it is grounded firmly in our value of faith, is expressed in and through our value of family. It's who we are, and that is reflected in the decisions we make, what we do, how we act, how we serve people, and how we engage the kingdom and the world. While that's true for us, though, I know it may not be true for you. For many, the word *family* isn't exactly a source of warm, fuzzy feelings or tender memories. Our families have the potential to bring out our best . . . or our worst. With all this in mind, let's take a look at what it means to live with a family value focused on the family itself.

WHAT IS A FAMILY?

The word *family* is used to describe a lot of different relationships these days. We might talk about our family, our family of friends, our work family, our church family, or our neighborhood family. In fact, you can call *any* group of people you know through a specific point of contact your "<BLANK> family." When we were serving as missionaries in Brazil, for instance, we were thousands of miles away from home and made many close, personal, lifelong connections with people who became like brothers and sisters to John and me and aunts, uncles, and grandparents to our children. During that season, when visits home to the States were rare and before technology gave us cheap and reliable phone and video-call capabilities, that "family" in Brazil was incredibly important to us. In fact, we've been home from Brazil for almost thirty years at this point, but just last month I spent six fun weeks with one of my best friends from there. We'll always be connected, and she and my other friends from there mean the world to me.

However, when we talk about *family* here, in the context of our family values, we're talking about the very special, unique collection of people God has brought together under your roof. According to God's design, the heart of that family should be a loving marriage between a man and a woman. Genesis recounts, "Then the LORD God said, 'It is not good for the man to be alone. I will make a helper who is just right for him.' . . . This explains why a man leaves his father and mother and is joined to his wife, and the two are united into one" (Genesis 2:18, 24, NLT). Children are the miracles who spring forth out of that marriage (either by birth or adoption), filling our homes with laughter, excitement, sorrow, stress, and new dimensions of both joy and anxiety that the young couple had never previously imagined.

That's what I think of when I hear the word *family*. Now, is that a perfect definition? No, probably not. Are there healthy families that don't look exactly like this? Absolutely. I believe God is always in the business of shaping and molding us into something else. Who and what we are today—either individually or as a family—is not who and what we will be one, five, or twenty years from now. As God said through the prophet Jeremiah, "O Israel, can I not do to you as this potter has done to his clay? As the clay is in the potter's hand, so are you in my hand" (Jeremiah 18:6, NLT). God keeps us on the potter's wheel, spinning us round and round, shaping us, thinning a section here, adding more clay there, smoothing out a rough spot, pinching pieces off, and so on. So, your family will almost certainly look different from mine as God shapes each of us and each of our homes into something new.

No matter how different our families are, though, they all play a fundamental role in shaping us into the man or woman we are becoming. Furthermore, your family of origin will always hold a spot in your life that is distinct from any other group or community you are ever a part of—for better or for worse. Some people with difficult or abusive family backgrounds might resist this, and that's perfectly understandable. When you're young, you don't have a lot of say about who your family is. This changes as you get older and start making your own decisions. You can choose to engage more fully in your family, or you can choose to wholly separate yourself from all or parts of it.

Even though you can't do much to change your family when you're a young child, you certainly do have full control over your family dynamic when you're an adult. You don't choose the family you're born into, but you do choose the family you're creating as an adult. You choose your spouse, you raise your children, you set the family values, priorities, and so on. That means *your* family—the one you're responsible for building—can be whatever you want it to be. You get to decide how your family acts, what you believe, where you go, what you do, and what's important to you. What a huge responsibility! Every one of those decisions is an investment you're making in the next generation. Families build communities, and communities build societies. You're literally shaping the world of tomorrow by the family you're building today. Later in this book, we will explore some strategies for strengthening your family bonds by sharing intentional, planned value experiences together. For now, let's focus on what truly makes a family a *family:* the marriage and children at the heart of it.

MARRIAGE: THE HEART OF THE FAMILY

"Trudy, what kind of man do you think you'll want to marry when you grow up?"

I was thirteen years old, and my father and I were taking a walk on the beach during our summer vacation. I told him quite honestly that I had no idea. After all, I had never even been on a date with a boy at that point! He smiled and said, "It's never too soon to start thinking about this, you know. One day, you are going to make a decision that's going to affect you for the rest of your life. I think that's something you need to prepare for."

My parents had taught twelve- and thirteen-year-old boys and girls in Sunday school for most of my life, and I'd heard them talk about "The Three Ms" a thousand times. They always stressed to these teenagers the need to get serious about their Master, their Mate, and their Mission—the three most important decisions they'd ever make. Apparently, age thirteen is when Dad wanted me to start thinking about my *mate,* which he always stressed would be the second most important relationship in my life (second only to my relationship with Christ). He encouraged me that day to start talking to the Lord about it and to identify a list of qualities, physical traits, personality traits, and values I hoped to find in a husband someday. So, I did just that.

I jotted down a few things on a piece of paper and tucked it away in my Bible. Over the next several years, I would often pull it out, review it, write more things down, and erase other things. I would add something else and then, after praying about it, realize that what I had just added wasn't important. The list was always in progress. It matured as I did. But it was valuable because it always had me thinking about who I wanted to spend my life with. By the time I graduated high school, I had a good mental image of the type of man I hoped to meet and marry.

Soon after arriving at Samford University as a freshman, I started dating a young man I met there. We were together for a few months, and it was clear we were pretty interested in each other. Then one night, he told me about some unwise decisions he had made when he was in high school. That was tough information to hear because eighteen-year-old Trudy didn't know how to process it. I went back to my dorm room and pulled out that piece of paper from my Bible. If this list truly identified the man I wanted to spend my life with, I knew I had a problem. The guy I'd been seeing had broken some of the commitments I had decided were extremely important to me. I had to pray through that. I had to search my heart and God's will for whether these were unfair or overly idealistic expectations or if this really was something I wanted and expected a man to live up to.

After wrestling with it for a little while, I was convinced I needed to break it off with that young man. He was a good person, and I was certainly able to forgive him for the things he had done before we had ever met. That wasn't the issue. The issue was that I had made some commitments to God about who I was waiting for, and it was time for me to put up or shut up. Eventually, we broke up, I met John not too long after that, and the rest is history. Because of that, John has always liked to joke about how important that list was to his life. I didn't realize it all those years while I was working on it, but I was making that list just as much for him as I was for me. If it weren't for that list, we might not be together today. And neither one of us can imagine a life where we aren't together!

Young, In Love, and Immature

Just because John and I can't imagine being with anyone else after all these years doesn't mean we've had the perfect marriage. We haven't. The truth is, there is no perfect marriage because there are no perfect people. I was only nineteen when we met. I was away from home and operating my own Chick-fil-A restaurant at the time, so I'm sure I felt pretty grown-up. But anyone older than thirty knows *no one* is fully grown at age nineteen! I still had so much to learn about the world, about relationships, and certainly about myself. Fortunately, John was willing to go on that journey with me.

Early in our marriage, although we were both fully committed to our relationship, we butted heads quite a few times. We were very young, fairly immature, and selfish. And, I'm ashamed to say, when either of us didn't get our way, we would have a huge, blowout argument in our little apartment.

I'll never forget one night in particular. We were really at each other's throats about something (I have no idea what), and the argument was dragging on. Neither of us was willing to give an inch of ground. In anger and desperation, still trying to "win" the argument, I said, "John, this is the way it's going to be, and if you don't like it, I'll just leave and move back in with my parents!"

It wasn't long before the full weight of those words hit me like a ton of bricks. I thought, *Did I really just say that? Am I willing to end my marriage over this silly argument?* No! It was a childish outburst, an empty threat. But the fact that those words actually came out of my mouth scared me. It scared John too. That argument forced us to confront our immaturity and selfishness.

Fortunately, cooler heads prevailed, and John and I came together for some important, prayerful, level-headed discussions. We agreed to never talk to each other like that or make those kinds of threats again. We pledged that we would not use divorce or separation as a threat or leverage to get our way. Leaving home was never going to be an option for either of us. We were committed to our marriage and, even when things got difficult, we promised each other we'd stick it out and work toward healthy solutions.

And, with God's help, we've kept that promise for forty-five years and counting! We haven't had that kind of argument in a long, long time. Sure, we still argue even after four decades together, but we do so in a respectful, loving, and (hopefully) mature way ... at least most of the time!

Keeping the Right Focus

Your marriage is the beating heart of your family. Sure, it can often feel like your children are front and center, but it's your spouse who was with you at the beginning and who will be with you till the end. At this point in our lives, John and I have spent more time living together *without* children in the house than we did *with* children in the house. If your entire family revolves around your children, what do you think will happen when they are grown and gone? What will be left of your intimate, one-on-one relationship with your spouse when it's just the two of you knocking around your big, empty, quiet house when the last child leaves?

There were times in our marriage when I was so focused on the children that I admit I lost sight of my husband a little bit. John had to remind me many times that God gave me *him* before He gave me children. Fortunately, God blessed me with a patient husband who was bold enough to remind me that we needed to work hard on our relationship apart from the children. And now, looking back, we see that the greatest gift we gave our children—the greatest gift any parents can give their children—was a strong, healthy, vibrant, active marriage!

Much of what we will discuss in the later chapters of this book can and should be applied to the family as a whole—parents and children together—but please do not neglect your marriage. Take time together, focus on each other, invest in your relationship, and never stop growing in the Lord individually and together. Take advantage of date nights and marriage retreats whenever you can, even when you have little ones at home screaming for your time and attention. You and your spouse need each other, and you need each other *for life*. Prioritizing your marriage is hands-down the best way to maintain a family value of family.

LIFE'S GREATEST CALLING

Ever since I was a little girl, I have known in my heart that my greatest calling in life was to be a wife and mother. Everything else I've ever done—operating a Chick-fil-A, serving as a missionary, being a camp director, writing, public speaking, and so on—has been a distant second at best to this primary calling. I became a wife at age twenty-one and a mother at twenty-four, and I've spent the last forty-five years trying to grow and mature in these roles. I haven't quite figured it all out yet, but I'm getting there!

I firmly believe that children are a gift straight from the hand of God. They are a *blessing*. Of course, that blessing comes with a lot of hard work and a great deal of responsibility, and that responsibility never stops, no matter how old your children are. My four don't need me quite as much today as they did thirty years ago, but they still need me—and I need them. Plus, I now have the added blessing and responsibility of being a grandmother to so many incredible, energetic boys and girls. I've learned over the past eighteen years that all that time I spent parenting my children was just the basic training I needed to become a world-class Mimi to my grandchildren!

I'm sure my strong connection to the value of family goes back to my own childhood. I had a wonderful childhood with two parents who loved each other deeply and who poured that love out onto me and my two brothers. I've said much about my father, of course, but I think it's my mother who truly planted that strong sense of family in the core of my being. She was the best example of a godly wife and mother I could imagine. As a young girl, I remember watching how she loved and supported my father, took primary responsibility for raising three children, managed the household, ran the farm, served in church, and taught us all a deep, abiding love for God, music, and family. My mother was a tiny firecracker with boundless energy and an enormous spirit, and I have spent my whole life trying to be the kind of wife, mother, and now grandmother that she was.

But my mother wasn't perfect . . . and neither am I. Looking back, it's easy to see several times I got it wrong with my children. I gave them my all, but I, like every mother, fell short at times. John and I were often too demanding on our children. We were short with our words sometimes. We were often selfish with our time, not always giving them the one-on-one attention they needed. Sometimes, we expected them to act like adults even though they were young children, and that was understandably hard on them. We were both still so young, and we still had a lot of growing up to do ourselves.

We got several things right, however. We did learn to apologize to the children when we messed up, and we were very open with them that we were going to make some mistakes as parents. We also tried to include the children in the different things we were doing—a lesson I learned from my father. I practically grew up in the kitchen of my dad's restaurant. He let me and my brothers roam free wherever we wanted, so we knew every part of that building and business. I believe that early exposure is what gave us such a strong sense of connection to and emotional ownership of Chick-fil-A today. My father's restaurant wasn't just his job; it was our second home. I still get that same feeling walking into a Chick-fil-A restaurant or our Support Center in Atlanta.

While we were in Brazil, for instance, our children followed us around everywhere. They went with us when we visited people and worked on ministry projects. Of course, they were with us at church, and they were a big part of our ministry there. We often hosted people in groups at our home, and they would help us entertain them. They were such a big part of the relationships we were building there. We were intentional about including them, and we resisted the temptation to just ship our children out of the way whenever we needed to do something important at home. We looked for ways to include them, and I believe this gave them not only a stronger sense of family but a stronger sense of mission in the work we did together as a family.

In doing this, John and I lived out our value of family. We showed our children in real and practical ways that our family is a team. We live together, work together, play together, and serve together. We are each individuals, equipped by God with spiritual gifts, talents, interests, personalities, and passions, but we also fit together in a special way to operate in unison. Our goal has always been to discover not only what God wants *me* to do but what God wants *us* to do. We know He has a mission and a purpose for our family, and we have always strived to fulfill that purpose by being the strongest, tightest family unit possible.

Roots and Wings

As a parent, I've always tried to give my children two crucial things: roots and wings. When your children are young and in the home with you, you're helping them develop deep roots, which they'll need for stability as they grow up and eventually leave home. Those roots assure them that they are loved, valued, and uniquely gifted by God to do something magnificent in the world. These roots serve as "home base," giving them a place to belong, a place to "come home" to, and a stable platform from which to launch into the big, bold, amazing life God has in store for them as adults.

Then, once those roots are firmly planted in the foundations of faith and family, you have to focus on giving your children wings. This means preparing them to one day fly away into their own lives, trusting them to make their own decisions. This is where so many parents struggle. We often work so hard to create a safe place for them to grow up that we lose sight of the fact that, one day, those baby birds will need to leave the nest. Even though we may want to keep them with us forever, home safe with Mom and Dad, we realize (in our brains if not in our hearts) that our job as parents is to spend every moment we have with them preparing them for the day we let them go. And that can be much harder for the parent than it ever is for the child.

I used to see this play out on a small scale during my summers as a Camp Director when parents would drop off their children. Many parents would be more nervous and upset about dropping their children off than the children were about being away from home for a couple of weeks. I see this on a much greater scale these days when parents drop off their recent high school graduates at our nine-month Impact 360 Institute Fellows gap year program. This is like dropping your child off at college. One day your child lives at home with you, and the next they do not. Children and parents respond to this in different ways.

We were living in Richmond when our oldest went off to college, and she chose to go to Mississippi College, sixteen and a half hours away. Nobody prepared us for how hard it would be to drive off and leave her there, away from us, on her own, out in the world to do her own thing. That was so devastating to us. We had spent eighteen years building roots in our daughter, and now it was time to let her fly away. All we could do was pray that her wings were strong enough.

Our second child went to Auburn University in Alabama, and the third went to Union University in Tennessee. Both of those schools were far from Richmond as well. But we noticed it got easier each time we dropped a child off at school. In fact, by the time we dropped our youngest off at the University of Mobile in Alabama, we had gotten the hang of it. It was probably *too easy* for us, to be honest. We basically dropped him off at his dorm and then drove off for a beach vacation. Poor David called us as we were driving away, saying, "You didn't even take me to Walmart to get the supplies I needed! You just dumped me and flew off!" Maybe John and I had grown new wings of our own by then!

The roots are important because that's what's going to ground them in the storms of life, particularly if you've grounded them in the truth of God's Word. That's the foundation you *want* to give them, because when life gets tough, you don't want them running back to you; you want them running to the Lord. As you raise your children, you first teach them *parent*-control, then you move on to *self*-control, and finally you want to teach them *God*-control. That's the one that's going to stick with them and give them the best guidance for life.

As crucial as those roots are, though, you also can't neglect to build up their wings. It may be impossible to imagine if your little ones are still crawling around at your feet, but your children will eventually become adults, and adults have to be able to make their own decisions and be responsible for themselves once they leave home. And they *will* leave home... one way or another. I've heard that mother eagles gradually make their babies' nests more and more uncomfortable to encourage them to leave. Finally, she'll push the baby eagles out if it looks like they're getting too comfortable. If they stay in the nest, they'll never fly free and never be able to take care of themselves.

We live in a culture in which parents are trying to make it too easy for their children to stay home, thinking we're helping them by saving them from the weight of adult responsibilities. We're doing our children a disservice when we refuse to prepare them for adulthood and then fail to *force* them into adulthood by kicking them out of the nest (or off your insurance, or off your cell phone plan, etc.). We're doing too much to *protect* them and not enough to *prepare* them.

When we hover over them too much or too long, we might be trying to take the place of God in their lives. We should instead equip them for the life ahead of them and teach them to rely on God (not Mom and Dad) when life gets hard. We can protect them when they're in our homes, but we can't once they leave. The best we can do is to raise them to depend on the Lord and to call on Him in times of trouble. As the psalmist said, "But as for me, how good it is to be near God! I have made the Sovereign LORD my shelter, and I will tell everyone about the wonderful things you do" (Psalm 73:28, NLT).

Helping your children develop wings means giving them the freedom and opportunity to try new things—even though they may fail. That can be so frightening as a parent, and yet giving our children room to fail is one of the greatest gifts we can give them. My father trusted me with my own Chick-fil-A restaurant to operate when I was just nineteen years old. I was the youngest Operator in Chick-fil-A's history at that time. And don't for a second think that Truett Cathy gave his little girl any special treatment! Yes, he gave me the opportunity, but that included the opportunity to fail. He made it clear that I couldn't run straight to him for any special favors or protection if I got myself or my restaurant into a pinch. I was left to sink or swim just like any other Operator.

But here's the thing: the fact that my father trusted me enough to give me that opportunity, that he put his own name on the line in front of every employee and every other Operator in the entire company . . . it meant the world to me. I was nervous, of course, but even more than that, I was blessed with enormous wings of confidence that my parents had been developing in me for nineteen years. And then, when it was time, they set me free to fly. And guess what? I flew. So did you. And, believe it or not, so will your children and grand-children. That day is coming, so be sure you're always working on their wings as long as they're in the nest.

A WELL-WATERED GARDEN

So many things in the world are fighting for our attention that creating quiet space to focus on your family can seem impossible. Even if *family* isn't one of the top five values you select in the values cards exercise, do not fall into the trap of putting your family on the back burner of your life. Your family must always be a *priority*, even if it is not a core *value*.

That said, I know as well as anyone that family life isn't always beautiful and peaceful. It's often difficult, exhausting, and downright heartbreaking. There will be days when these people who mean more to you than anyone else will disappoint and hurt you. There may even be moments when you feel as though your children are pulling up the roots you worked so hard to plant in their lives and flying away from you on the wings you helped them build. Those are the days when your family life feels more like a barren desert than a lush, green garden. In those times, I encourage you to use *your* wings to fly straight into the arms of your heavenly Father. He is where you want your children to fly, and He is there for you as well. As the prophet Isaiah said so beautifully, "The LORD will guide you continually, giving you water when you are dry and restoring your strength. You will be like a well-watered garden, like an ever-flowing spring" (Isaiah 58:11, NLT). The Lord will nourish your soul, enabling you to get back to the good work of tending the garden of your family.

CHAPTER 5

OUR FAMILY VALUES #3: INTEGRITY

In 2021, about one year into the COVID-19 pandemic, I started having some issues with my neck. I was referred to a physical therapist twice a week for about twelve weeks. When we first got started, mask rules were in full effect, so the therapist who worked with me had to wear a mask and I had to wear a mask every time we

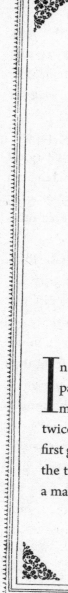

saw each other. I'm sure you remember what that strange season was like.

About eight weeks into my physical therapy, the mask requirements finally eased up a bit. I went in for my session one day, and she greeted me without a mask on. I remember standing there looking at her thinking, *Oh! That's what she really looks like!*

I had spent an hour with her twice a week for two months, but I had never seen her face. Even though we had built a great relationship the previous eight weeks, something shifted from that day forward. I felt like, for the first time, I *really knew* her and she *really knew* me. We were able to engage each other fully, having taken our masks off.

The reason I'm sharing this little story is that, sitting here thinking about our third family value, integrity, I'm taken by the fact that so many of us are wearing a different type of mask all the time: the mask of inauthenticity. We wear one face to work, another to church, another at home, and so on. It's like we keep a mask rack at our front door, and we grab the appropriate "look" we want to present to the world every time we leave the house. In the process, we're presenting a false—or, at best, *skewed*—view of who we are to the people we interact with. And, in doing so, we are not only being inauthentic; we're being unfaithful to God in covering up the true, wonderful, gifted, authentic man or woman He's made us to be. Today, perhaps more than ever, we need to take a step back and explore what it means to live out the value of integrity.

DEFINING INTEGRITY

We often experience a lot of pressure to create an image for ourselves of how we want people to see us. As a result, we often try to act *that way,* so that's the way they will see us instead of how we really are. As common and even as understandable as that is at times, it still represents a breakdown in integrity.

I define integrity as being the person God made you to be, no matter where you are or who you're with. It's about being real and authentic. Integrity and authenticity are a simple matter of just letting people know who you really are.

I've heard Rick Warren teach on this very topic, and I love how he explains that integrity is based on *wholeness.* The very word *integrity* comes from the Latin word *integer,* which means "whole" or "complete." Integrity, then, is the opposite of segregation; it's all about integration, a life that is completely and fully integrated. When you're living a life of integrity, you are whole. Who you are and how you act in different places and scenarios is consistent. Rather than dividing your life into categories, acting one way at home with your family and another way in public with your friends, for example, you are always simply *you.* There is no disunity in your personality, and your work friends, church friends, school friends, and family members all have a consistent experience of *who you are.*

I once heard about a family that went to church every Sunday morning. The parents were active in their Sunday school class, they served on the Welcome Team, and they sat right up front during worship. Everyone at church loved this family. One day, after the service, the pastor greeted them at the back door as they were leaving. As the couple spoke with the pastor, their young daughter tugged on his suit coat to get his attention. He smiled down at her when she said, "Pastor, I love it here! Is there any way my family could just move into the church and live here full time?"

The pastor laughed and said, "Oh, I don't think that would work out. Why on earth would you want to live inside the church building, anyway?"

With no hesitation, the child said, "Well, my parents act a whole lot nicer here than they do at home. I wish they could act like this all the time!"

Whenever I tell that joke in one of my speaking engagements, the crowd will laugh . . . but then there's a bit of an awkward silence. How many of us are quietly guilty of having that kind of separation between our "church selves" and our "home selves"? Too many, I'm afraid.

Doing the Right Thing for the Right Reasons

Although authenticity is important, integrity isn't *only* about being who God made you to be no matter where you are or who you're with. It's also about doing the right things for the right reasons. Taking it a step further, integrity is doing the right thing *even when no one is watching*. We often think about being cautious of how we do things when people are looking, but the real test is what we do when people aren't looking or listening. Does our behavior match our beliefs, and do those beliefs match God's principles and His Word?

Besides, from a faith perspective, someone is *always* watching. The apostle Paul admonished us, "Work willingly at whatever you do, as though you were working for the Lord rather than for people" (Colossians 3:23, NLT). We aren't doing it for applause or "attaboys;" we're doing the right thing *because* it is the right thing and because our heavenly Father is watching.

It is always better to please only God rather than get the applause of a thousand people. Jesus spoke directly to this:

> Don't be like the hypocrites who love to pray publicly on street corners and in the synagogues where everyone can see them. I tell you the truth, that is all the reward they will ever get. But when you pray, go away by yourself, shut the door behind you, and pray to your father in private. Then your Father, who sees everything, will reward you. (Matthew 6:5–6, NLT, emphasis added)

Ultimately, we answer to God, and He is the only audience who matters—*and* the only audience who sees every performance.

That said, it's important to understand that He is not some big, cosmic judge sitting on a throne in the sky waiting to condemn us. Instead, He's right there beside us, in every step and in every conversation, walking with us, talking to us, and helping us make the right decisions. Integrity and authenticity require us to walk closely with Him. I once heard someone illustrate this as two people walking closely enough to share an umbrella. As long as you're walking side by side with God, you remain under His umbrella of protection. However, when you get out of step with Him—or flat out walk away from Him—you become much more vulnerable to all kinds of attack.

A Good Reputation

I quoted Proverbs 22:1 in an early chapter, but I think it also applies here: "Choose a good reputation over great riches; being held in high esteem is better than silver or gold" (NLT). Other translations use the term *good name* rather than *reputation*, but I think *reputation* is especially fitting when we talk about integrity. Of course, our reputation is a reflection of what other people think about us—whether we have a "good name." And that reputation is based on their experience of us, or how we act and what we say when we're around them. We should absolutely strive to have a good reputation, but we should not do that just so everyone thinks well of us. Instead, that reputation has to be built on our true character, which is who we really are.

When we live with integrity and godly character, we can't help but have a good reputation. More importantly, that reputation is a true reflection of the man or woman God made each of us to be. We are pleasing Him by showing the world the unique beauty and giftedness He put within each of us. And, in so doing, we are building a good name, or reputation, for ourselves.

A FOUNDATION OF TRUTH AND TRUST

Integrity has to be based on the foundational idea that objective right and wrong *actually exist* and *can be known*. In other words, some actions and behaviors are good and some actions and behaviors are evil. There is an ultimate truth in the universe by which we measure what we understand to be right and wrong in daily life. This truth is objective in that it is based on something outside of ourselves and our individual preferences or desires. We can't simply *decide* what's right and wrong; instead, we have to *discover* it. Why? Because reality is involved. We understand that God is the ultimate source of what is true and what is good, and we can know what is right and wrong when we understand and obey His principles because they are rooted in His character and commands.

For most of my life, no one really questioned the fact that there is a common, universal truth in the universe. People understood that things like lying, stealing, destroying public property, and physical violence were *always* wrong. A wrong thing generally wasn't deemed right based solely on how the perpetrator felt about what they were doing. Right was right, wrong was wrong, and truth was truth. It wasn't very complicated.

Not so anymore.

Today, we live in a world that is always trying to revise right, wrong, and truth. People like to talk about "my truth" versus "your truth" or "what's right for me." The problem here is that truth is truth. If something is true—meaning that it accurately describes reality—then it is *always true*. When you take yourself out of the central position of defining what is true and measure objective truth against something bigger, purer, and better than yourself, you realize that "what's true" isn't up to you. But many people *can't* take themselves out of that central position. They refuse to recognize the existence of *the* truth—a universal standard that exists outside of themselves—and so they live their lives according to what they think, what they feel, what they want, and what they believe. And if someone else has an entirely opposite view? No problem. In today's world, two opposite things can both be true. That is, of course, until "their truth" collides with "your truth" and you are back at square one of appealing to a universal standard to settle the question. Not only is the "true for you but not for me" approach contradictory, it's also unlivable in everyday life.

When we try to view this through the lens of integrity, however, we have a problem. Integrity is based on a foundation of what is true and what is good. And if everyone has their own personalized, humanized, self-centered version of truth, then integrity as a known, shared value is built on an unstable foundation of shifting sand. It simply cannot be measured, cannot be transferred or taught, and cannot and will not stand up to any kind of storm. Without a basis in truth, there can be no integrity. Jesus said, "I am the way, the *truth*, and the life" (John 14:6, NLT, emphasis added).

Broken Trust, Broken Integrity

To illustrate this point, let me use an example that strikes a bit too close to home. Between the ages of six and eight, I must admit I had a problem with lying. It probably started as one of the few ways I had to get back at my two older brothers, but then it turned into a bad habit. For instance, I remember rummaging around in my mom's pantry one day when I accidentally broke a glass vase. My immediate thought was, *Oh no! I am going to be in big trouble. I've got to figure out how to get out of this.*

Before anyone else had a chance to see the broken vase, I immediately went to my mother and blamed the broken vase on one of my brothers. I said, "He is never going to admit to this, but Dan just broke that glass vase in your pantry. I'm sure he'll deny it when you say something, but he broke it." Of course, Dan didn't know anything about it. He denied it when my mom asked him about it, and he probably got punished for lying to her on top of breaking the vase—even though he did neither.

I'm not proud of this, but I got pretty good at lying with a straight face. It became very easy for me to blame things on other people. Eventually, my parents caught on to what was happening. There were many times when I would tell my parents something, and they honestly didn't know if they could believe me or not. Many times, my father would look at me and say, "Now, Trudy, are you really telling me the truth?" It always hurt when my father doubted my word—even when I knew I was lying to his face!

Looking back all these years later, especially after becoming a parent and grandparent myself, I realize it probably hurt my father a lot more than it hurt me to have to ask me that question. For the longest time, I couldn't even imagine how disappointed he had been with me every time he knew I was lying to him. Until, that is, I got to experience his side of things quite unexpectedly one day when I was watching one of my grandchildren.

A granddaughter was spending the day with me, and I realized that she had eaten something she wasn't supposed to. I asked her about it and, just like her grandmother had done fifty years earlier, she looked me right in the eyes and told me that she had not eaten it. It was obvious that she had, however. Part of it was still smeared on her mouth and cheek!

I gave her every opportunity to tell me the truth, but she never did. I know sneaking a piece of candy might seem trivial, but this experience really scared me. I was looking into the precious face of a child I loved more than anything, realizing that she could lie so well to me with a straight face. My mind immediately went back to my own lying when I was young. I thought about how I did not want to see that in my grandchildren, and I worried what that little seed of lying could potentially grow into as she grew up.

I've thought about that experience quite a bit over the years, and I continue to pray for this grandchild. Even though she is a wonderful young lady and certainly very trustworthy today, it's hard to forget something like that. Small as the lie might have been, I realized she had broken my trust for the first time, and that is difficult to get over at any age.

Few things destroy a person's integrity—not to mention others' trust in them—like being caught in a lie or breaking one's promises. In fact, I'd argue that broken promises are the number one cause of bitterness in the lives of children. We teach integrity by doing what we say we will do, but broken promises create bitterness, mistrust, and insecurity. There is just no way to sugarcoat it: failing to live up to your word is a breakdown in integrity. Whether it's coming from a child, parent, or grandparent, broken promises cause a lack of trust, and broken trust can be very difficult to recover.

For example, if you consistently fail to pick up your child when you said you would, you're actively teaching them not to trust you. This further teaches them that your word has no value, and you're showing them with your actions that you lack integrity, that there is not *wholeness* in your character. In chapter 3, we saw Jonathan Morrow's definition of faith as *active trust in something you have a reasonable belief is true.* When you give someone good reason *not* to believe what you say is true, they will understandably stop putting active faith in what you say. Put simply, they'll stop believing in you.

We cannot allow that to happen, especially with our children and grandchildren! So, if you say you're going to do something, do it—even when it comes to something the child *wishes* you'd forget, like discipline. Think about how many times you have seen a child misbehaving in the grocery store and overheard the parent say something like, "That's it! You're going to be punished when we get home." Now, how often do you think that parent actually follows through with that promise of punishment by the time they get home and unpack the groceries? Not often, I imagine. Of course, the child in that situation is happy every time Mom or Dad "forgets" the punishment, but there's a problem here. If you don't follow through with that consequence (or promise), you're teaching the child not to believe you when you say they'd better stop misbehaving. They know there will be no future punishment because you've taught them that you'll forget by the time you get home.

More importantly, when you fail to keep your word to your children, you're showing them that God cannot be trusted to keep His word either. You are the earthly representative of their heavenly Father. That is an awesome, somber responsibility. Children will learn to trust God (or not trust God) by learning to trust (or not to trust) their earthly parents. In this, few things are more important in parenting (and grandparenting) than living a life of integrity for and in front of your children—*every single day.*

Consistency Is Key

One of the key factors of integrity is living a consistent lifestyle. When we are living out who God created us to be and doing the right things for the right reasons, and when we do that over time, we are consistent. Our children and grandchildren will certainly *see* what we do occasionally, but they will truly *know us* by what they see us do day in and day out over the course of our lives. That's how we show them who we really are—by what they see us consistently doing and what they hear us consistently saying.

When I talk about living a consistent life, I can't help but think about my father. He was a very, very busy man—long before he was ever the CEO of a multibillion-dollar company. When I was a young girl, I saw my father every day in all his roles. He was a Christian, husband, father, uncle, brother, business owner, Sunday school teacher, and community leader. He invited us into his office when we were little, even if he was in the middle of an important meeting. He delivered a fresh lemon pie from his restaurant to a different person who needed a little encouragement almost every day on his way home from work. He went to the Georgia Baptist Children's Home regularly to pick up a carful of orphan boys and bring them back to our farm to play. He was a lot of fun and loved making people laugh, whether he was at home, work, or church and whether or not the people around him knew who he was. Everyone he ever interacted with knew the *same* Truett Cathy. There was no disparity between who he was or how he acted, regardless of which "hat" he was wearing at any given time. My father taught me that it's okay to wear a lot of different hats, but all those hats need to go on the same head. That is, your roles may change, but *you* never should. A life of integrity means that everyone gets to see and know the same version of you.

Proverbs 11:20 declares, "The LORD detests people with crooked hearts, but he delights in those with integrity" (NLT). Our hearts are *crooked* when our words, actions, and attitude are always changing direction, but we live with integrity when they're straight, consistent, and whole.

John and I realized an inconsistency in our life a few years ago, and the instant we saw we were saying one thing *here* and another thing *there*, we knew we had to make a change. It's well known that Chick-fil-A is closed on Sundays. Many people still don't understand our commitment to that principle, but it has always been and will always be a nonnegotiable issue for us. Some estimates indicate that Chick-fil-A would become up to 15 percent more profitable literally overnight if we opened on Sundays, but that's never going to happen. Why? Because from the early days of my father's first restaurant, he committed to staying closed on Sundays. His restaurant was open twenty-four hours a day, six days a week—and he worked like crazy every one of those six days— but he personally loved spending Sundays with his family. We went to church together, had lunch together, played together in the afternoons, and had friends and family over to visit at night. And, of course, Dad would usually take a nap at some point, gathering his strength for the week ahead. Those Sundays were precious to us, and Dad always wanted his employees to have that same consistent experience with their own families and churches. So, from day one, he kept the restaurant closed on Sundays. It wasn't because it was a "churchy" thing to do; it was because he valued the freedom to spend Sundays in worship and with his family. And besides that, he was exhausted and needed rest.

I've been explaining (and sometimes defending) that position for more than sixty years, but somehow, an inconsistency snuck into my life that John and I discovered and knew we had to correct. We built our current home on my parents' property, which includes the farm and farmland I grew up on. With that, we employ a handful of full-time employees who are dedicated to the farm and property. If you know anything about a farm, you know there is work to be done every day, especially if you have farm animals. The problem we recognized is that some of our guys were working a few hours on Sundays, taking care of feeding the cows and horses. When

John and I realized the inconsistency of having these good men work on Sundays while our family is known for giving employees Sundays off, we had to make an immediate change. We met with the crew, told them they were going to have Sundays off effective immediately, and worked with them to come up with whatever plans were necessary to ensure the animals had what they needed for that day without the crew. It certainly wasn't an impossible problem to solve; it's just one that, I'm embarrassed to say, snuck past us for a little while.

Now, you might read that and think we were being a little too legalistic with our stance on working on Sundays, but for us, it just comes back to consistency. If it were truly a value of our family that our employees should have Sundays off, we knew we needed to be true to that value across the board, whether we were talking about restaurant employees or farm employees. We want everyone, whether they work with us at Chick-fil-A or work with us at the farm, to get the same experience we have. We believe that consistency is a critical piece of our integrity. Otherwise, people could rightly accuse us of doing one thing in public and another thing at home. So, we'll do everything we can to honor God and honor our family values by living lives of integrity—even if it means the cows have to eat day-old grass once a week!

TEACHING INTEGRITY

When it comes to teaching integrity to our children and grandchildren, John and I have started by admitting to them that we are not perfect (as if they hadn't figured that out on their own).

We do not get it right every time. I think it's important that they realize our own lives are a work in progress and that God is working in our hearts to perfect us, just as He is working in their hearts to perfect them. But we are not perfect now, and we never will be on this side of heaven. When you go back through the Bible and see stories about David, Noah, Moses, Abraham, and all the people God used, you see they were certainly not perfect either. But they sought the Lord, and that is what we are striving to do in our own lives.

The Example You're Setting

As I've said before, parents should be more concerned with the example they're setting for their children than they are the words they actually say to them. Again, more is caught than taught—and this can have both good and bad consequences in a child's life. Even if the parents tell their children not to lie with their words, for instance, their actions will speak ten times louder. Children can't help but think, *If it's okay for them, why is it not okay for me?*

Here's an example that may strike close to home: When our children were growing up, we didn't have cell phones. We were like most families in that we had a landline and one phone number for the whole family. If a teenager answered the phone and the caller asked to speak to their mother, the child would put the phone down, find his mother, and tell her that she had a phone call. Now, what happened if the mother in this example didn't want to talk to the caller? She might have said, "I don't want to talk to that person right now. Just tell them I am not home." How many of us have heard a parent say something like that?

Of course, the mother might have said this without really thinking about it, but what message would that have sent to the child? Not only is the teen seeing his parent lie, but the parent is asking the child to lie on her behalf. Again, this is about your *actions,* not your *instructions.* You can tell the child not to lie all day long, but then if you *ask them to lie for you,* they will see what you really think about the importance of telling the truth. Instruction is what we *say*, but influence is what we *do.*

Parents have a biblical duty to model and teach integrity to their children. Proverbs 20:7 says, "The godly walk with integrity; blessed are their children who follow them" (NLT). I have no doubt that my family has been "blessed" because of the integrity of my mom and dad. That motivates me that much more to hold this value in high regard in my own family. And I'm especially blessed that my children have married such wonderful spouses who are equally committed to demonstrating integrity to their children. My oldest grand-child, Ashlynn, recently commented to me that she has never heard her father talk negatively or critically about another person. What an amazing thing for a child to say about her parent! Can you even imagine that? But her father, Trent, has been intentional throughout her entire life about acting with integrity and in a Christlike manner. By watching her father live out this wonderful life of integrity, Ashlynn's life has been forever changed. She'll never forget the impact her father has had on her life, just as I could never forget or outgrow the impact my own parents had on mine. And, as a grandparent, it is an enormous blessing to watch my son-in-law take such a wonderful, godly, active role in modeling Christlikeness to our grandchild.

Integrity Requires Clarity

For a child to grow up respecting and modeling integrity, the parent must set and enforce clear guidelines. Integrity absolutely requires clarity. Children need to know what the boundaries are so they can know how to avoid crossing them.

Lack of clarity leads only to frustration. This is true in our homes and in our businesses, and it's true in our personal walks with the Lord. Just think about it: if God was not clear in what He asked of us and what He commanded in His principles and teachings, or if He was wishy-washy and His truth changed from circumstance to circumstance, you would be totally frustrated all the time. You could not have a fulfilling, meaningful, significant life because you would never know what you should and should not be doing.

In the same way, when we do not establish clear guidelines for our children, they will likely feel as though they can never please you *or* God, because they will never know what the standard—the objective truth—is. A family value of integrity requires clarity, boundaries, and, when lines are crossed, correction. Further, these things must be taught, maintained, modeled by the parents, and enforced. Without putting these things in place and being consistent in demonstrating them in front of the children, a parent is inconsistent and unclear. You cannot have integrity while being inconsistent and unclear about what you believe to be right, and you can't expect your children to value what they don't see you valuing yourself.

WHAT WOULD JESUS DO?

When my children were young, the WWJD—"What would Jesus do?"—craze hit the scene in a big way. You don't see it nearly as much these days, and it may even seem trite to you if you remember seeing WWJD emblazoned on everything from T-shirts to bumper stickers to shoestrings. But I have always thought WWJD is a great rule of thumb for knowing when, where, and how to act with integrity. Sometimes, when you're struggling with the temptation to have a momentary lapse in integrity, the best thing you can do is take a breath, take a step back from the situation, and honestly ask yourself, "What *would* Jesus do in this situation?"

The result, I think, is the type of person described in Psalm 15:

Who may worship in your sanctuary, LORD? Who may enter your presence on your holy hill? Those who lead blameless lives and do what is right, speaking the truth from sincere hearts. Those who refuse to gossip or harm their neighbors or speak evil of their friends. Those who despise flagrant sinners, and honor the faithful followers of the LORD, and keep their promises even when it hurts. Those who lend money without charging interest, and who cannot be bribed to lie about the innocent. Such people will stand firm forever. (Psalm 15:1–5, NLT)

I think that this passage sums up everything I pray we have taught our children about living lives of integrity. And it's who and what I'm still striving to become myself.

CHAPTER 6

OUR FAMILY VALUES #4: GENEROSITY

Every Sunday, it was the same routine. We all piled into the car—Mom and Dad in front and us three children in the back—and headed to church. As soon as my mother got settled in her seat and Dad pulled out of the driveway, I'd always see Mom reach into her purse, pull out her checkbook, and write out a check. It was my parents' tithe, and it served as a vivid reminder to me as a little girl that my parents were committed to giving a portion of everything they earned back to God. Seeing that check in her hand every week is my earliest, most enduring memory of generosity in action, and it has become the bedrock of a family value of generosity that has marked the Cathy and White families for as long as I can remember.

My mother was serious about giving. Long before I ever saw those tithe checks in her hand each week, the value of generosity was so important that Mom wouldn't even accept Dad's marriage proposal until she was certain they were on the same page about money and lifelong giving. When he proposed, she did not say yes right away. He was twenty-seven years old and only two years into running his business, at that time a single little diner, which he and his brother Ben had taken out a partial bank loan to open. I often wondered as a young girl why she didn't accept his proposal immediately. Then, one day, she told me. It was because she had to be absolutely sure that he was committed to tithing his income, no matter how much or how little it was. She was uncomfortable with the idea of marrying a man who might not share her value of giving in obedience to the Lord. It wasn't about legalism or simply following the rules. It was about making sure she married a man with a generous heart. Fortunately, my father was just as committed as she was. From the first day of their marriage, they were a perfect partnership of generous giving.

I saw tithing in action every week, but I don't remember my parents ever sitting me down and actually teaching me the importance of tithing or giving. As we've seen often throughout this book, this was an example of something being *caught* rather than *taught*. Also, I didn't have much money of my own as a young child. My parents didn't pay us for chores we did around the house very often, which I guess is pretty common for children who grow up on a farm. I got my first job working as a lifeguard when I was a junior in high school. When I got my first paycheck, I knew 10 percent of that would be going to my church that week. It was automatic. I didn't even think about it or make a conscious decision to give. In my mind, that was just what you did. I'm sure my parents discussed their giving among themselves; from my perspective, I just saw my mom writing that check in the car every week of my life as a child. Even after my dad passed away, my mother sat down to calculate what their weekly tithe should be. She had it all mapped out on notepaper. I've left those notes still sitting in her desk drawer, years after her death. All that to say, when I started having an income of my own, it was perfectly natural for me to give a tithe to the church.

The same is true for John. He grew up watching his parents tithe and talk about the importance of giving his whole life. So, when he got his first job bagging groceries at the local grocery store, he started tithing his own income just as I had. Again, it wasn't some big, grand decision that both of us made. We were merely doing what we had seen our parents do.

I am so grateful for the example of my parents. Because I had grown up seeing it, I never once struggled with writing that check. I knew deep in my heart that none of the money I "had" belonged to me. All of it was God's (Psalm 24:1), and He had called me to give a portion of what was already His back to Him. Even though it was there on my paycheck, I knew it was the Lord's.

Speaking to the Ephesian leaders in the book of Acts, Paul declared, "I have been a constant example of how you can help those in need by working hard. You should remember the words of the Lord Jesus: 'It is more blessed to give than to receive'" (Acts 20:35, NLT). This is a hard concept to teach children. Even as an adult, it can be difficult to understand that you are going to get much more satisfaction out of your *giving* than you will from *receiving*. And yet, a lifestyle of generosity goes hand in hand with a life of faith. Even if you don't specify generosity as one of your personal family values, it is something that we're all called to prioritize. But, contrary to what many believe, *generosity* does not necessarily mean giving *money*. Let's look at what it means to live with a value of generosity.

DEFINING GENEROSITY

Generosity starts with the understanding that God owns it all. The psalmist declared, "The earth is the LORD's, and everything in it. The world and all its people belong to him" (Psalm 24:1, NLT). That means God is literally the owner of everything in the universe. He made it all, and it all belongs to Him. So, whatever we have is either given to us *by* God or is merely on loan *from* God. Whether it's in our pockets, our homes, or our bank accounts; whether it's the hours we have in a day or the days we have in a year; or whether it's the talents, skills, and experience we each have in abundance—it's ultimately

His. Therefore, this whole concept of generosity is simply the act of being a good steward—or manager—of what God has entrusted to us. As such, the key question around generosity is simply, "What does God want me to do with what He has entrusted to me?"

Sometimes in defining a word, it helps to look at its opposite. The opposite of generosity is stinginess or hoarding. It is holding everything for yourself. It is the belief that God cannot meet my needs, so I must hold on to everything tightly so that I can provide for myself and my family instead of taking a step of faith and saying that I can actually trust God. When we are stingy or maintain an attitude of hoarding, we're essentially saying, "God has given me these things, but I cannot trust Him to help me understand how to use them and how to manage them well." And so, we take full control (or at least partial control). We assume total ownership rather than keeping our proper perspective as simple managers of these things.

This attitude betrays a heart problem, and the heart is at the very core of a generous life. We often think generosity is all about how much we have to give, whether it's time, talent, or money. But that isn't true at all. Generosity is not about how much you have; it's about your willingness to give—whatever that means in your specific, unique situation. It's an attitude of the heart. God never puts a limit on how much is "enough," whether it's how much wealth is enough, how much service is enough, how much talent is enough, or how much giving is enough. Frankly, God isn't all that concerned with the amounts; He is more concerned with the generosity of our hearts. If He were to put a specific amount or percentage on what's "enough" to give, then everyone would just strive to meet that amount to "check the box." That makes our giving more of a rule than an outgrowth of a healthy, vibrant, trusting relationship with the Lord.

But God is focused on the relationship, not the amount. Hebrews 11:6 says, "It is impossible to please God without faith. Anyone who wants to come to him must believe that God exists and that he rewards those who sincerely seek him" (NLT). When we try to "impress" God with the big number on our giving, we're missing the point. It's about the heart of the giver, not the size of the gift. Scripture says, "For God loves a person who gives cheerfully" (2 Corinthians 9:7, NLT). Therefore, we get it wrong both when we hoard and when we exaggerate our giving, trying to impress God. The right attitude in giving should be, "Am I willing by faith to put this before the Lord? What is the right provision for me, and what has He given me that should be shared with others?"

In writing to the Philippians, the apostle Paul declared, "I know how to live on almost nothing or with everything. I have learned the secret of living in every situation, whether it is with a full stomach or empty, with plenty or little" (Philippians 4:12, NLT). We should all strive to achieve that level of maturity when it comes to our worldly possessions. Paul knew it is up to God to determine how much to give us. That's not our responsibility. Our responsibility is to *manage* whatever He *does* choose to give us. Whether that is a lot or a little, we have to decide how to manage it in a way that is pleasing to Him. The goal here is not perfectly calculating the amounts but focusing on the contentment at the center of it all.

The Beginning of Gratitude

Both generosity and gratitude are family values for us, but I always place generosity before gratitude when listing or explaining them. Why? Because generosity is the *beginning* of gratitude. Generosity forces us to move away from doing only what makes ourselves comfortable and move closer toward becoming dependent on God. When we hold loosely with open hands on to what He has given us, we are showing faith that He will provide more when we need it. We don't have to cling to what we have today, because we know He will be with us tomorrow as well.

This is the lesson God was trying to teach the Israelites during their wandering in the desert:

> Then the LORD said to Moses, "Look, I'm going to rain down food from heaven for you. Each day the people can go out and pick up as much food as they need for that day. I will test them in this to see whether or not they will follow my instructions." (Exodus 16:4, NLT)

God provided quail and manna for food every day, and He told the people to collect only what they needed for *that* day. They learned every morning that God was still with them, providing for them.

In *God Owns It All*, author Ron Blue argues that generous giving breaks the power of money in our lives.[3] An unwillingness to give reveals our discontentment and lack of trust in God. We are scared to give because we are scared He won't provide more for us in the future. We think we cannot afford to give because we have gotten used to living on more than we make. The truth is, if you are not willing to give, you are unable to live a contented life because you're fixated on what money is going to provide. You're looking for comfort, security, success, fame, recognition, or something else instead of being content with God. As such, you are focused on the *gifts* rather than the *giver*. Giving disrupts that mentality.

Giving is an acknowledgment of our dependency on the Lord. By giving generously, we proclaim, "I can give this freely because I trust the God who delivered it to me, and I can trust Him to do it again." What a marvelous expression of faith! And no, this is certainly not a "give in order to get" mindset. I'm not saying God *rewards* our giving by giving us even more in return. But I am saying that God *honors* our giving. When He sees us living in faith and putting our trust in *Him* rather than in the money He's entrusted to us, we show Him that we can be trusted with more—if that is His will for us. Maybe it is, maybe it isn't. That's not for us to decide. All we can do is show ourselves to be trustworthy stewards of whatever He puts in our hands.

FOUR AREAS OF GENEROSITY

We usually think of money when we talk about generosity, but money is only one part of it. There are other things we can be generous with, and those can be just as important as money.

That's great news! Because generosity isn't about money, this means *anyone* can be exceedingly generous. When we served in Brazil, for example, we were surrounded by a community of people who didn't have much in terms of financial wealth, but they were unbelievably generous with the resources they *did* have. They were the perfect examples of what the Bible means when it says, "God has given each of you a gift from his great variety of spiritual gifts. Use them well to serve one another" (1 Peter 4:10, NLT). Simply put, generosity can be as easy as using whatever gifts you have to make other people feel loved.

Specifically, John and I like to focus our giving decisions on four key areas:

1. **Time:** This is the one resource everyone gets in equal amounts. No one is wealthier or poorer with time than anyone else. We all get the same amount; the only difference is how we each choose to use it.

2. **Talents:** God has uniquely gifted each of us with special talents, and those talents must be managed and shared just as intentionally as our money.

3. **Resources:** Money is certainly a resource (and an important one), but it's not our *only* resource. How can we steward our relationships, personal network, education, life experiences, and so on in a way that serves others and honors God?

4. **Opportunities of Influence:** How can we make the most of each opportunity to leverage our influence, using each one as a way to bless others and expand the kingdom?

When you look at giving through this lens, it becomes clear that money just might be the easiest thing to give!

Of all the things we have to give, I think time can be the trickiest. Time is the one thing we all have in equal amounts, yet it's the one thing we all seem to need more of. However, how often do we overcommit ourselves, giving our time to things we are not especially interested in or gifted at? I can't tell you how many times I've been sitting in a meeting or serving on a committee and thought, *What in the world am I doing here?*

Giving our time is never "convenient." Giving away our time to someone or something else is always a sacrifice; there is always something else we could be doing with that time. But there can also be great rewards that come from this sacrifice. It's like an investment. A financial investment costs you something up front, but then (hopefully) you and others can reap more than you sowed. When it comes to investing time, that reward usually comes back in the form of lives touched. That can certainly be more difficult to measure, but it is exponentially more gratifying!

As with any investment, you want to give your time wisely. Whenever I give my time to something, I want to be sure of the following:

- I'm maximizing that investment by giving them my very best.
- I'm not wasting my time on something I'm not especially gifted or called to do.
- I'm not taking up a seat that would be much better filled by someone else.

Now, it may sound strange to sift your service opportunities through such a practical, pragmatic filter, but trust me, this still leaves *plenty* of things for me to do. And the best part is, I can always be sure that the people and organizations I donate my time to get the very best of me!

One way I give of my time is by sending personal emails to Chick-fil-A support staff and Operators who have had a big life event, such as a death in the family or the arrival of a new child. We receive these updates as prayer requests in the Support Center, and my assistant sorts through them and makes a list of people and prayer needs for me. Then, I spend some time each week going through them, praying for them by name, and writing a personal email to them to express my condolences or congratulations. I also keep track of special days in the lives of our family and friends, such as birthdays and wedding anniversaries. I file them by date and pull a week's worth out at a time. I'll pray for the person and then write a note of encouragement and drop it in the mail. I'm always amazed by how much people appreciate these small acts. People need to know that others "see" them and pray for them, and simply getting a note to that effect can change the whole course of someone's day!

Sometimes, though, gifts of time might be less planned and more spontaneous. Those can be fun too. For instance, new neighbors moved in down the street recently. I've popped in on them a couple of times to meet them and welcome them to the area. Recently, I was driving home from my office around lunchtime, and a random thought popped into my head: *Maybe I should take lunch to my new neighbors.* I had already passed the nearest Chick-fil-A (my go-to lunch option, of course!), and I was almost home. Would it be convenient to turn around and drive back to pick up some food? No, not really. It would take an extra twenty or thirty minutes, in fact. However, I just felt like it was the neighborly thing to do, so I turned around, drove back to Chick-fil-A, bought a few meals (yes, my family does *pay* for our food at Chick-fil-A!), and then drove back toward the house. The young mother and her daughter were so surprised and grateful when they saw me standing there with a big bag of food! This neighbor had had a rough morning, and it turned out that the Lord put them on my heart at the perfect time. She really appreciated it, but to be honest, I think I got as much or more out of it than she did! I love it when God uses me to be a blessing to His children!

GUIDELINES FOR GIVING

While the point of these chapters about my personal family values is to provide an example about how you can articulate and focus on your *own* family values, I simply cannot miss this opportunity to share some important "guidelines for giving" that have shaped how John and I have expressed our value of generosity over the years. Giving has been a fundamental part of my life since childhood, as my parents modeled generosity even when Dad was the struggling owner of a single restaurant way back in the 1940s. And sadly, I've learned the hard way that a heart for giving can lead to unexpected trouble if you aren't clear about how to *manage* your giving. Here are a handful of guidelines that have served us well.

Spouses Must Work Together on Giving Decisions

First and foremost, if you're married, you must work with your spouse on all your big giving decisions. Your spouse is your helpmate, the person God specifically gave you to help carry your burdens. The Bible explains marriage as a "one flesh" relationship in which two people become one. When either of you makes a big decision without engaging with the other, you're using only half your brain! Your spouse is not here to frustrate you but to complement you. We need to look at giving opportunities from all angles, and spouses help us see the different perspectives we might otherwise miss.

Our family often gets requests to help with a variety of needs. And because we strive to be good stewards of all the blessings God has given us, we take every opportunity seriously. But we do it as a team. We go to the Lord to discuss potential opportunities to give and to find out what God wants us, as a family, to do in response. Sometimes we both feel Him telling us to help. Sometimes we don't. And then sometimes one of us will feel more inclined to help than the other does. Those are the times when we have to dig in a bit more and figure out how to get on the same page.

Of course, even when we both feel God leading us to help in a particular area, we still have to work together to determine *how much* help God is calling us to provide. Sometimes, when we are trying to decide on the amount to give, we will each write a number on a sheet of paper so we don't influence the other's thinking right off the bat. Oftentimes we're pretty close. Other times, we're far apart. That's okay. That just gets the discussion started, and then we work together to figure out the right answer.

While this process certainly keeps us in sync with our financial giving, we also depend on it to make our giving decisions when it comes to our time, talent, and opportunities of influence. We do this when one of us is asked to serve on a committee or an organization's board, when we're invited to attend or lead events, when we're asked to mentor or disciple someone, when we have the opportunity to host someone or a group in our home, and so on. John and I are committed to staying in sync on *all* our giving—not just financial—and that is one of the most important parts of our marriage.

These discussions about when, where, how, and how much to give are some of the richest, most rewarding talks John and I ever have. These opportunities can make you and your spouse truly feel like a team that God has put together. Yes, this can lead to some disagreements, but the bottom line is that we do not make giving decisions without the consent of the other. This one guideline has probably been the most important principle we've followed regarding our giving.

Narrow Your Giving

The second most important principle has probably been our discipline in narrowing our giving. That may sound surprising in a chapter about generosity, but the plain fact is that no one can serve *every* good cause. If you try, you'll just throw a dollar here and an hour there, and that won't be much help to anyone. Instead, we recommend narrowing your giving into a few key areas that are especially meaningful for you.

Our three key focus areas of giving are as follows:

- Alleviate risk to children.
- Develop followers of Jesus.
- Reach the nations with the gospel.

This isn't *all* the giving we do, but the bulk of our giving—probably 90 percent or more—is focused on these three areas. This gives us more clarity when we are evaluating an opportunity to give our time or money. If we're approached with an opportunity from an overseas orphanage, for instance, we know we'll consider that much more seriously than we might take an environmental charity. It's not that the environmental cause is less important; it's just that we have identified as a family what is specifically important to us, and we like to focus our giving in those areas as much as possible to help ensure we're taking care of the causes God has placed on our hearts.

Now, do we occasionally give to causes outside of these three areas? Of course! I like Girl Scout cookies as much as the next person! But we aren't going to go all-in on something outside our three key areas. We do, however, have a fourth giving bucket we call "Unexpected Opportunities." That's what we use to cover any giving opportunities we feel called to support that fall outside our primary focus areas.

Knowing what matters to us provides guardrails to help focus our giving, and that's especially important when it comes to saying no to a good cause. Again, you can't support every charity, so identify what you specifically care about and point your giving dollars in that direction.

Be Specific and Intentional

The best kind of giving is specifically tailored to the other person's needs or preferences. That's why it's always a good idea to really get to know the person or organization you plan on giving to. This can be as easy as a simple questionnaire. For example, John and I try to stay connected to the students attending the nine-month gap year program we founded several years ago. This is a group of students age eighteen to twenty who embark on an adventurous year of intensive equipping that includes biblical worldview studies and leadership training, along with an immersive international experience. This year strengthens their spiritual formation as they move forward with their traditional college education. This is the first occasion most of these students have ever been away from home for any length of time, and it's important to me to get to know each of them in a personal way, even though I'm not there on campus with them every day.

Several years ago, I got the idea of creating a questionnaire for incoming students that asked them about their favorite candy, hobby, colors, and general interests. Then, throughout the year, I create customized care packages for each student, filling the box with exactly the things they told me they liked. That makes each box unique and, more importantly, uniquely customized for each student. When they receive these care packages, they've told me it's like getting a package from home because it's full of their favorite things.

I shared this recently with a friend who is a former VP of a big company. He said he used to do something similar with his employees. As part of each new team member's onboarding process, his assistant sent them a questionnaire asking about their favorite candy, stores, restaurants, movies, hobbies, and so on. Then, whenever he wanted to do something special for an employee, he could simply pick something off their list and surprise them with it. It was a great way to support the people who worked so hard for him.

It's a special blessing to be on the receiving end of such a thoughtful gift. Just last week as I write this, I spoke at a training event with those who serve in different areas of volunteer leadership for summer camp. They presented me with a small gift as a token of appreciation. It was my very own Nesquik (formerly Nestlé Quik) tumbler for mixing chocolate milk. Now, you should understand that I absolutely love chocolate milk. It's one of my favorite things in the world. What made this little gift so special is not just that they gave me something *I* knew I would enjoy; they gave me something *they* knew I would enjoy. They had taken the time to get to know my personal likes and dislikes, and they went to the trouble of picking out a little something for me. That kind of personalization means the world.

When you know exactly what someone enjoys, it doesn't take much to make them feel special and uniquely appreciated. It isn't about spending a lot of money on someone. It is about making the best use of whatever you choose to spend.

In cases like these, just a small token can make a big difference in someone's day.

Plan Your Giving for the Year

Something we've found surprisingly helpful—especially now that our family has grown so large with so many wonderful grandchildren—is planning our giving for the year. Remember, generosity isn't *only* about stewarding money; you're also trying to give your time, talent, and opportunities of influence. These can be difficult decisions if you're trying to make them on the fly. Life gets pretty crazy for most of us, so it's best not to leave your giving decisions to chance or to your whims in the heat of the moment.

For that reason, John and I sit down with our calendar once a year and block out time specifically for acts of generosity throughout the year. First priority are our children, their spouses, and our grandchildren. We make sure we not only have all their birthdays and major ministry commitments accounted for but also that we're planning appropriately for the handful of times we will all be together during the year (which we'll discuss in later chapters).

This might not sound especially relevant when it comes to being generous, but I promise it is crucial. We have four children, four sons- and daughters-in-law, and sixteen grandchildren. That's twenty-four birthdays alone to keep track of! If we weren't intentional about keeping track of all this, we'd miss something. Besides, being intentional about calendaring our time for them is one way we show how much we love them. They know we're serious about giving our time to them because they see it planned months in advance on our family calendar.

This type of planning is also crucial when it comes to budgeting our giving. It's important for families to know when any big expense is coming, even if that "expense" is a financial gift to your church or a charity. For instance, you might "adopt" a family or two at Christmas, providing gifts for underprivileged children and Christmas dinner for their family. That's a wonderful way to show the love of Christ, but it takes planning. Similarly, you need to budget your family's time. After all, your time is a fixed resource; none of us have more than twenty-four hours a day to work with! Looking at the year ahead enables us to block off whole days, weekends, or weeks that we can dedicate to joining in ministry and service projects, leading workshops, volunteering at church, and participating in other opportunities to give our time, talents, and opportunities of influence.

You don't want a beautiful act of generosity to wreck your own family's budget, eat up your precious family time, or leave you personally exhausted and overcommitted, so make sure all these things are laid out on the calendar and in your budget well in advance.

Fund Your Children's Giving When Necessary

Teaching young children how to give can be tricky, especially since they don't often have much money of their own. Whenever possible, then, we recommend funding their giving by giving them money and teaching them how to use it generously for others.

For example, we took a family trip to Honduras a few years ago. We like to take a family trip once a year to invest in creating memories—a great use of time and money. Some years that trip is a vacation, and some years it is dedicated missionary or service-oriented projects (which we'll discuss more later). Before we left, John and I got all the grandchildren together and explained to them that we would encounter many poor, under-privileged children on our trip. We discussed what things they might need, whether it was toys, clothes, hygiene products, and so on, and then we gave each of them a certain amount of money. Then, we took them all to Walmart before we left town with the goal of using that money to buy something they thought the children in Honduras would need. That way, even though they were using *our money*, they were using *their own time* to help bless the children of Honduras. We wanted to show them that giving isn't just about money; it's also about how we use our time, attention, and effort to be a blessing to others.

Teach Children How to Be Generous with Their Words

One aspect of giving that often goes unnoticed is how to be generous with our words. Being generous in our speech—such as with encouragements, thanks, compliments, and words of support and affirmation—is something anyone can do, regardless of who they are, how old they are, where they live, or how much they have.

For example, John and I host a three-day overnight camp experience for our grandchildren every year called Camp MiPa. One of the ground rules for Camp MiPa is that our words have to be positive and encouraging. That means we do not allow the children to whine, complain, or tattle on their siblings or cousins. To be honest, the children don't always like this rule. Oftentimes, a child will come up to us and start telling us this or that. I'll have to look down and cut them off, saying, "Wait a minute. Is what you're about to tell me positive and encouraging?" That's about when they huff a little bit, roll their eyes, say "no, ma'am," and then wander off.

We don't ignore legitimate problems or concerns, of course, but we do cut off any unnecessarily negative chatter. This is a minor blessing in the short term and an unbelievable blessing in the long term. After all, teaching children how to be gracious and generous with their words is one of the greatest gifts you can give their future spouse!

Progressively Involve Your Children as They Get Older

Involve your children in giving opportunities that are appropriate for their age. When they're very young, for instance, you should let them engage in specific, narrow ways they can more easily understand. For example, when we first moved to Brazil, none of us could speak the language very well. That made it difficult for us to truly become part of the community and get to know their needs. However, two very obvious needs in the community near us were poverty and hunger. So, one of the first things we did to get to know our neighbors was cook a huge pot of rice and beef stew. Our plan was to go throughout the community and offer our new neighbors a free meal for their family.

Our daughter Joy was four at that time. I explained to her what we were going to do. I said, "Today is Saturday, and we're going to go to the people around us who are very hungry. One of the best things we can do for them right now is give them food. So, Dad and I are going to take them a meal. It is one way we can show them that Jesus loves them even though we can't speak to them very well yet."

Joy had a huge heart even at that young age, and she wanted to be able to do something to help us. So, she wrote "Jesus loves you" in Portuguese on dozens of pieces of paper. Then, she went out into the community with us. Whenever we gave someone a bowl of stew, she greeted them with a big smile and put that note in their hand. I actually have a picture of Joy at four years old handing someone this note on the streets of Brazil. That has become one of my favorite memories.

This experience had a huge impact on Joy. Simply involving her in what we were doing enabled her to catch a vision for what it looks like to be generous. You can *talk about it* all day long, but when you actually *do it* and let your children come alongside you and do it with you, that's when the lesson really takes root. As I've said many times, more is caught than taught.

Years later, when our children were in high school and college, we began to have more detailed conversations with them about the different causes we gave to, why we chose those causes, how often we gave, and so on. We didn't share amounts with them at that point; we just wanted them to understand what causes and ministries our family had chosen to support and why. We had some very open discussions with them at that point.

Once they were out of college and starting their careers, John and I expanded their involvement by asking for their input in our giving decisions. We asked them to help us identify different causes within our primary key giving areas and to help research the different charities that popped up. This had the surprising effect of opening up our giving in all new ways. Our children identified some fantastic ministries and charities we had never heard of. We're so grateful for our children's involvement because some of our favorite organizations are ones we would have otherwise missed. Utilizing our children's insight and personal networks expanded our giving in wonderful, dramatic ways. Plus, it made our giving much more personally fulfilling because it was something we were doing together with our children.

As our children graduated from college, started their careers, and began investing in giving initiatives of their own, John and I set up a special fund designed exclusively for matching their giving dollars. This was just one more way we not only incentivized their giving but also discovered new, exciting ministries we might potentially support ourselves. You don't have to match dollar-for-dollar, and you might even match with your time, talents, or opportunities of influence instead of with your money. We have to get out of this mindset that "giving means money." It doesn't! Your gifts of time, talents, and influence can be just as significant—often more significant—than any dollar amount. If you can match your children's giving in any way, to support them and to discover new ministries and causes, we've found this is a great way to give your children one final push into the wonderful world of generous giving as adults.

Do Due Diligence

So often, people make their giving decisions at the drop of a dime, simply reacting to different needs that pop up or that the news media is pushing. There's certainly a place for reactive giving, but that cannot and should not make up the bulk of your financial generosity. Instead, you should treat your acts of giving like an investment. Just because a charity sounds good doesn't mean it is. Sadly, many nonprofit organizations are poorly run at best. When you make a financial gift to a charity, you want to know your money is actually going to help the people the organization says they serve, not to fund endless red tape in their corporate office or, worse, to help the founder buy a second jet. Not to sound negative, but we've all seen such horror stories in the news in recent years.

While I strongly encourage you to give generously, I do not want you to give *blindly*. Dig in, get to know the organization and/or the specific project you're giving to, look at how they spend their money, find out how much of their donations go to people in need versus "administrative costs," and give wisely. The money you give away will be some of the most important investments you ever make, because you're investing in the kingdom of God and in the lives of His children. Don't throw your money away on organizations that will either waste or pocket your donations.

Do Your Giving While You're Living

So much of our giving is traditionally tied up in our dying (i.e., our estate plans). It is a wonderful thing to leave your wealth to the people and causes you cherish, but don't save it all for after your death. Give while you're still living to see the blessings of your giving in action.

This occurred to us once we started taking our estate planning seriously. We didn't like the notion that the bulk of our giving would take place after we were dead, so we changed things up and started implementing our giving while we're still here to see it and to play a role in managing the giving in a hands-on way.

THE BIG DEBATE: GIVING IN PUBLIC OR IN PRIVATE?

I've never been comfortable doing a lot of giving "out in the open." John and I have mostly followed the Matthew 6:3 principle: "When you give to someone in need, don't let your left hand know what your right hand is doing" (NLT). That is, don't make a big show of your act of giving. I'd say we have done this for the vast majority of our giving—especially our financial giving—for two good reasons:

- It's what the Bible tells us to do (Matthew 6:3).
- So that God (not us) gets all the glory.

This policy has worked well for us in general, but we've more recently been challenged to use our giving as a way to inspire *others* to give. And that has indeed been a bit of a challenge for us.

Sometimes, you do things that nobody else is going to see. But other times, you might consider how your own giving might encourage others to give. They may see your generosity and think, "That looks amazing! Could I ever do something like that?" They might not give in the exact same way, but they may wonder, "How can I do something special for others and find joy in giving like this person has?"

Seeing the power of someone giving can and does influence us to step up our own giving. Besides, some projects are simply too big for any one giver to fully support. Many initiatives need a great deal of support, and having a few public donors can inspire and encourage many others to join the effort. This also opens the door to other options, such as donor matching. This isn't about everyone giving the same amount; that almost never happens, because each person is in a different financial situation. We shouldn't strive for equal *amounts* but for equal *sacrifice*. One family might give $1 million. Another family could make an equal sacrifice and give $1,000. Again, it's not about the amount; it's about the heart of giving.

When you give openly, you have the opportunity to make it known that you believe the money is the Lord's and that He has given it to you to manage. You can keep the focus on Him and make it clear that you view yourself only as the channel through which He is giving this gift. Making that known can be a huge incentive for others, and it's a win-win-win for you, the other giver, and the cause you're both supporting—as long as you keep your heart humble and focused on the Lord.

That said, there's still nothing quite like the fun of anonymously leaving a $100 tip on a $10 restaurant bill and running out the door before the server knows what's happening!

CHAPTER 7

OUR FAMILY VALUES #5: GRATITUDE

Our whole world seems to be built on the idea of instant gratification. More and more, we are being taught from birth that we can have anything we want anytime we want it. Despite my best efforts, I have felt this mentality creeping into my own life. Take Amazon, for instance. Amazon has conditioned us to expect any product at a great price delivered to our door the next day. If I'm ordering something from Amazon and see that it will arrive a week later, I feel that little spark in my brain that says, "What? A whole week? That's ridiculous! Why can't I have it *now*?" When I stop to think about it, of course, I'm reminded that it's practically miraculous that I can have most items delivered in less than a week. That's certainly a big change for those of us who still remember what it was like when our shopping was restricted to only what we found sitting on store shelves on any given day!

But it's not just shopping that's teaching us impatience and, if I'm being honest, a bit of entitlement. Just last week, a friend was telling us about a trip his family took to Disney World this year. They have recently changed their ticketing and park features, and we asked him how it went. He said, "It was weird. When I was a child, I remember there being one line. There weren't all these special access features that you could buy on top of your ticket. Even when I went a couple of years ago, there was still a *regular* lane but also a *fast lane* for people who had reserved a spot in line. Now, however, there is no 'regular' line. There is the 'Lightning Lane' and the 'Standby Lane.' All the signage on all the rides reflected that. It's like they're really going out of their way to make you feel special if you paid extra for faster access and like a loser if you didn't. By calling the *regular* line the *standby* lane, what they're really doing is telling park guests either 'Come on in right now!' or 'We'll get to you eventually. Maybe.'"

This endless need for more "stuff" and immediate gratification creates nothing but stress and anxiety for most people. And, as crazy as it sounds, this problem is thousands of years old. My guess is that people have felt this emptiness in their hearts from the moment sin entered the world. Two thousand years ago, Jesus was already having to talk people down from their anxiety about attaining more and more stuff:

> That is why I tell you not to worry about everyday life—whether you have enough food and drink, or enough clothes to wear. Isn't life more than food, and your body more than clothing? Look at the birds. They don't plant or harvest or store food in barns, for your heavenly Father feeds them. And aren't you far more valuable to him than they are? Can all your worries add a single moment to your life? And why worry about your clothing? Look at the lilies of the field and how they grow. They don't work or make their clothing, yet Solomon in all his glory was not dressed as beautifully as they are. And if God cares so wonderfully for wildflowers that are here today and thrown into the fire tomorrow, he will certainly care for you. Why do you have so little faith?
>
> So don't worry about these things, saying, "What will we eat? What will we drink? What will we wear?" These things dominate the thoughts of unbelievers, but your heavenly Father already knows all your needs. Seek the Kingdom of God above all else, and live righteously, and he will give you everything you need.
>
> So don't worry about tomorrow, for tomorrow will bring its own worries. Today's trouble is enough for today. (Matthew 6:25–34, NLT)

Strange how this ancient message sounds particularly well suited for our modern world in which unbelievable advances in technology and communication have seemed to make our lives more stressful, not less.

But how do we learn to rid ourselves of the stress and anxiety of today's (and yesterday's) *gotta-have-it-and-have-it-now* way of life? I propose that the answer is not to have *more* but to have *less*. And, more importantly, to be more grateful for what you do have.

Gratitude is the secret ingredient to a rich, full, generous, satisfying, and overall enjoyable life. But it doesn't necessarily come easily, and it may not come naturally. As we'll see, gratitude isn't just a value; it's a skill we must develop intentionally over time. John and I were both blessed with parents who knew the value of simplicity and gratitude, and that's a value that has been central to our family life since the day we were married. While all the White family values we've discussed are precious to us—just as I'm sure the handful of values you've identified for your family are precious to you—I believe it is gratitude that does the most to bring sweetness and satisfaction to our daily lives.

GRATITUDE VS. MATERIALISM

At its core, gratitude is just an expression of being thankful for and acknowledging everything God has put into your hands—big or small, "good" or "bad." It is an expression of thanks for how God works in and through all things in your life, even those things that hurt. It is, quite simply, the ability to stop, reflect on what the Lord has put before you, and say, "Thank You, Lord, for this blessing/trial/experience. I see You at work in this. In this and every situation, Your grace is enough for me."

Sadly, stopping to say thanks can be harder than it sounds, and honestly, saying, "Your grace is enough for me" can seem downright impossible for two big reasons: First, we usually don't want to express gratitude for the heartbreaking experiences we all face. We'll discuss this more fully below. And second, in a world in which materialism is running rampant, being able to say *anything* is "enough" is becoming far too rare.

Perhaps even more than grief and suffering, materialism is the true enemy of gratitude. This is true no matter how much or how little someone has. If you have a nice apartment and a bicycle, you want a home and a car. If you own a home and one car, you want a bigger home and two cars. If you make $50,000, you want to earn $100,000. Then, when you're finally making $100,000, you want $150,000. We spend all our time, effort, and energy in the endless pursuit of *more*. More money. More possessions. More power. More prestige. More friends. More toys. More distractions. More entertainment. More, more, more. The shame of it all is that our hearts will *never* be satisfied with the things of the world—we weren't designed to be satisfied with "stuff." But sadly, that's all some people ever chase. It's the nature of the human heart to want more.

We earn to spend. When we earn more, we spend more. We never reach a place that we can call "enough." Sometimes, getting more actually leaves us with *less* because our consumption outpaces our income. Or, as financial expert Dave Ramsey often jokes, "How many people do you know who celebrate a $400 per month pay raise with a new $600 per month car payment?" That's bad math! That pay raise actually leaves you with $200 less per month!

John and I have worked hard to focus on gratitude and contentment in our lives throughout our marriage—from our early days in a tiny apartment and struggling to pay our bills to our time serving in some of Brazil's poorest communities to today as we strive to be godly stewards of the immense blessings God has poured on our family. We have strived to live a life that reflects the life of the original Christian missionary, the apostle Paul, who wrote, "I know what it is to be in need, and I know what it is to have plenty. I have learned the secret of being content in any and every situation, whether well fed or hungry, whether living in plenty or in want" (Philippians 4:12, NIV). The funny thing is, we've found it is often easier to express contentment and gratitude in those times we've spent "in want."

You see, even when you are "living in plenty," as Paul says, your eye may still be wandering, scanning the horizon for the next big thing. A friend of ours, who is a self-described technology geek, often sighs as he shows us his new phone or laptop and says, "There's always an upgrade." His wife gets frustrated with him every Christmas because he is impossible to shop for. But that's not because there aren't plenty of good gifts she could get him; it's because he already buys everything for himself as soon as he can. Once the new model computer, tablet, smart watch, or cell phone comes out each year, he suddenly "realizes" the one he has isn't good enough anymore. Even my husband, the best person I know, struggles with this. There have been many Christmases I've been so frustrated because he's already snapped up what I was planning to put under the tree for him!

In his excellent book, *An Unhurried Life: Following Jesus' Rhythms of Work and Rest*, Alan Fadling writes, "Materialism sees gratitude as inefficient, diminishing our opportunity to take credit for achievements and accomplishments that God has enabled in our life."[4] That is so true. Gratitude for what we *have* and for what we have *done* is greatly diminished when we cannot stop thinking about what we want next.

GRATEFUL FOR THE HARD TIMES

It can feel so easy and natural to thank God for the happy times, those times when we feel on top of the world, "too blessed to be stressed," or, as people like to say on social media, #blessed. But what about those times when the *last* thing we feel like saying is "thank you"? During happy times, we can forget there's a much more challenging call for us in God's Word, which is to be thankful for even the difficulties we walk through.

Again, the apostle Paul models how to show gratitude in the face of adversity. In 2 Corinthians, he alludes to a personal struggle that largely remains a mystery to this day. He calls it "a thorn in my flesh, a messenger from Satan to torment me and keep me from becoming proud" (2 Corinthians 12:7, NLT). Some have speculated this could have been a chronic health issue, recurring pain, a speech impediment, or one of a number of other possible struggles. The truth is, it doesn't matter what exactly Paul was dealing with. In fact, I like that it isn't clear in the text, because it allows us to inject ourselves and our own struggles into Paul's words. We all know what it is like to constantly struggle with a "thorn in the flesh," some adversity that rises up against us, some tragedy that breaks our hearts, some loss that hits us out of the blue and threatens to throw our lives—not to mention our faith—off track.

Paul described how he prayed fervently on three separate occasions for God to relieve him of his source of pain, but watch how God responded:

> Three different times I begged the Lord to take it away.
> Each time he said, "My grace is all you need. My power
> works best in weakness." So now I am glad to boast
> about my weaknesses, so that the power of Christ can
> work through me. That's why I take pleasure in my
> weaknesses, and in the insults, hardships, persecutions,
> and troubles that I suffer for Christ. For when I am
> weak, then I am strong. (2 Corinthians 12:8–10, NLT)

What a powerful lesson to us today. It is amazing how relevant this timeless Word of truth is two thousand years later, when all the comforts of the modern world still leave us utterly dependent on God's loving care. Whatever we are going through, whatever pain we are experiencing, God is saying to us, "My grace is all you need." And for that, we can be grateful.

When I wrote my book *Climb Every Mountain*, I mentioned many of the difficulties I've had to go through in my own life. I'm sure you have a similar list. We all go through challenges and losses, such as the loss of a job, the loss of a relationship, or challenges between parents and children. We go through unexpected challenges with our health and with the health of people we love and care about. We experience the death of a loved one. Whatever the loss or difficulty is, it is hard to maintain a sense of gratitude in the face of all the hopes and dreams and aspirations we had for something or someone that we now know will not come to pass.

These are all challenges we can identify with and relate to. But these are also opportunities to learn more about *who God is* and *who we are* deep in our core. Even when our heart is broken—and sometimes *especially* when our heart is broken—we can and should be grateful for what God is still doing in our lives and what He is bringing about through our difficulties.

Too often, however, we tend to do the opposite: we turn and run away from the Lord and the church in the middle of a crisis rather than running toward Him and a family of believers who can help us. I think this is largely a result of an unwillingness to express gratitude for the hard times we face. Pain often closes us off from the world and even from God. When John was going through a frightening cancer experience a few years ago, he didn't even like to say the word *cancer* out loud. It took some effort for him to tell people what he was going through, because his inclination was to keep it to himself and to stay closed off. This extended into his worship experiences as well. There were times when we were in church that John didn't necessarily *feel* like praising God. Sometimes, singing the lyrics to a praise and worship song felt disingenuous to him. It took a little time for him to realize he wasn't paying attention to all the incredible things God was doing throughout his ordeal—the important conversations it inspired, the extra effort he put into engaging in his closest relationships, the new perspective it gave him and our family on what's truly important, and dozens of other blessings that weren't hidden, per se, but were instead sitting just beneath the surface.

When he was able to accept each of these things as a gift from God, his whole perspective about his cancer changed. Did that make my husband's cancer a "good" thing? Certainly not. But it did remind him—and those of us who love him—that God had not left or forsaken us.

If we don't understand the value of being grateful in both the good times and the bad times, then the tendency is to blame God for the difficulty rather than praise Him in the storm. This lesson has never been more important to us than it has been the past two weeks as I write this. I am actually working on this chapter a week later than planned. Rather than working on it last Friday, as I had scheduled, I spent that day grieving with my family and preparing for a funeral. Our youngest son, David, and his wife, Ashley, lost a child who died in utero. She was twenty-two weeks through the pregnancy with their second child when her doctor broke the news during a regular checkup that the baby's heart was no longer beating. This was a devastating loss for them and our entire family. Doctors induced labor a few days later, and our sixteenth grandchild—Carter Timothy White—was born only to be told goodbye.

I have been overwhelmed by David and Ashley's faith as they have walked through this nightmare. Even while grieving the loss of her son, whom we will never get to know in this life, Ashley remarked, "I know God is in control. But sometimes, I have to say it out loud so I can continue to believe it." She was expressing in a powerful way what John had learned through his cancer: that developing and maintaining an attitude of gratitude often requires a conscious decision and, sometimes, a semi-begrudging act of will.

Why "semi-begrudging"? Because it is so very difficult— it might even feel impossible—to express sincere gratitude *in the middle* of a crisis or loss. But we can at least be honest with God about where we are. The best we may be able to do in the middle of adversity is to pray, "Lord, my heart is breaking over this. And I admit to You that it is difficult for me to see Your hand or Your blessings in this storm. But I know You have promised to never leave us or forsake us (Hebrews 13:5). I know Your word says that all things work for good for those who love You (Romans 8:28). And I do love You. I want to be grateful for all things, but I need Your help. Would You please give me a heart of gratitude in this season?"

Time and distance help remove the sting of our suffering, enabling us to reflect on the unexpected blessings that come through it. Gratitude can do the same thing. Sincere expression of gratitude can release us from the pain of our suffering. We don't have to live there. We don't have to stay there. We don't have to be paralyzed by the pain. Gratitude can help you move through it and strengthen your confidence that the Lord will not only see you through it but also protect you from experiencing more than He knows you can bear.

Gratitude is leading us to live and abide in a state of contentment with the Father. He has our best interest in mind, even when we don't know what that might be. We do not know why we lost our grandson, Carter. We will never know this side of heaven, but the Father knows. Already in this short time, we are seeing glimpses of how God is receiving glory through this loss. God is using Carter's life and his death to accomplish His greater plan. That may seem impossible to us, but God sees things outside of time. His eternal vision enables Him to see this loss in the context of eternity—an eternity that we will spend with our grandson. We are hurting and missing him today, but God is reminding us that we'll have endless tomorrows with him in our future. And this is how we're learning even now to experience heartfelt, meaningful, sincere gratitude—even when we don't "feel" like it and/or when our external circumstances have brought us tragedy.

TEACHING THE VALUE OF GRATITUDE

Gratitude can be one of the most difficult things to teach a child, but I always wanted our children to grow into men and women who were thankful—thankful for the simplest of things. Raising them in Brazil made this much easier. I sometimes still wonder how typical children growing up in the comforts of America ever learn gratitude at all. Many children today simply don't have the perspective to understand how blessed they truly are. It is so difficult to teach gratitude and basic thankfulness in a culture that is so ready, willing, and able to throw all kinds of resources at us. With this in mind, how can we break through the cultural barriers and instill a strong value of gratitude in our children? I have a few tips.

Change Their Perspective Abroad

Frankly, I think one of the biggest blessings in my family's life is that we were able to raise our children overseas in Brazil. That made such a huge impact on our overall sense of gratitude because here in America, it can be easy to overlook the big and small blessings God puts in our lives, especially when our basic needs are being met so well. But raising our children in Brazil gave us a completely different perspective on what it meant to have "enough." Many of my children's friends' homes, where they'd often visit to play or spend the night, even had dirt floors. Can you even imagine your child understanding how blessed they are to have a simple wooden floor under their feet? It was a joy to raise our children there, where we could be grateful for the most basic things of life, like food, water, and shelter, that too many people take for granted in the modern world.

This experience gave all of us a wonderful new perspective and made us appreciate the simple things in life. For example, we take warm or hot water for granted here in the United States. However, the only way we were able to take warm showers in Brazil was with a special showerhead that had a tiny electric heater in it. Cold water passed through the showerhead and warmed up (a bit) before raining down on us. If the showerhead wasn't working correctly, we were stuck with a cold shower.

As was common with most homes in Brazil, our home also did not have central heating or air conditioning. During the cold season, we had a small portable heater that we rolled around from room to room in order to keep warm. During the summer, we had only portable fans to provide relief from the summer heat. Most of the people in our community did not have a car to drive. The members of our church walked there every Sunday. The dirt roads were so dirty and dusty that most people wore sandals for walking and then put on their "nicer" shoes when they arrived at the church. These were usually the only two pair of shoes most of them had.

Something as simple as a Ziploc sandwich bag became a huge blessing for us while we were in Brazil. We had never even considered this for a moment, but resealable sandwich bags simply did not exist in Brazil. At least when we were there, they weren't available in any stores. This is a big difference from most American grocery stores that have rows and rows of different sizes and shapes of resealable bags. For someone who had grown up with these bags, figuring out how to store things without them became an unexpected challenge.

Whenever someone from the States sent something to us, I always asked them if they could slip a Ziploc bag into the envelope. If they sent a package, I asked if they could throw a handful in. Whenever we were back in the States and then returned to Brazil, I always double-bagged everything as a way to bring extra bags back with me.

But simply *getting* them wasn't the only challenge. Once I had them, I did everything I could to *keep* them as long as possible. Whenever I used one, I rinsed it out and hung it to drip-dry so I could reuse it. I would keep using the same bag over and over again until it finally got a hole in it.

After we had been back home in the States for a while, I remember visiting with a friend in her kitchen while she was doing some simple chores. I stood dumbfounded as I watched her take something out of a sandwich bag and then throw the bag away. I was horrified! It was quite a readjustment to get used to seeing these things as disposable, because they had become so precious to me for the past ten years. I was always so grateful for every single bag that I couldn't imagine throwing one away so thoughtlessly.

Change Their Perspective at Home

I believe it's important to expose your children to the hardships of other people's lives so they can get a true perspective on what they have in their own lives. An international mission trip can be one of the best ways to do this, but you don't have to leave the country to reframe your thinking. It can be as easy as serving at a local shelter or simply taking advantage of the daily opportunities you have to broaden your child's view.

I was discussing this issue with a friend recently, and she mentioned a short exchange she had with her thirteen-year-old daughter. They were driving home from vacation, which took them through some new areas the child wasn't accustomed to seeing. My friend heard from the back seat, "Hey, Mom, look at that guy pushing a grocery cart down the sidewalk. Where is he going?"

Looking out the side window, my friend saw a poor, disheveled man who appeared to be in his fifties pushing a "borrowed" grocery cart filled with an assortment of obviously old, well-worn items, including a dirty blanket, a winter coat, and a little wooden stool. She then had to explain to her daughter that the grocery cart probably contained everything that person owned. This observation opened the door for them to have a very real conversation about homelessness and how blessed they were to have a home, a car, and to even be able to take a vacation.

So many children get a bad reputation for being spoiled or entitled. I am sure that this is true for many, but certainly not for all, young people today. I think the real problem is simply a lack of perspective. It's not necessarily about being spoiled; it's about not seeing how blessed they really are. And oftentimes, the children can't *see* because they aren't being *shown*. Being mindful about showing gratitude and thanks for everything we have, big and small, good or bad, helps break through this blindness and gives us a wider sense of the world. So, take an active role in broadening your child's perspective. Don't just give them things; talk to them about how those things should be seen as blessings in their lives. Help them understand that the remarkable blessings God puts into our hands—from good health to loving families to comfortable homes to an abundance of "stuff"—are truly gifts from the Lord and should not be taken for granted.

The Fine Art of Writing Thank-You Notes

One way my parents taught me to express gratitude was through writing thank-you notes. My mother and John's mother were both big proponents of sending handwritten thank-you notes whenever someone gave us a gift or did something special for us. Thank-you notes are a simple expression of recognition and appreciation that someone has given you something or taken time out of their day to do something nice for you. You always want to acknowledge that and express gratitude for it, and thank-you notes are the perfect way to do that. Sadly, though, sending thoughtful thank-you notes is becoming a lost art these days.

Not so with my mother. She used to buy *stacks* of cards at a time. In fact, when she passed away, I found a whole stockpile of blank cards that she hadn't used yet. She was very intentional about organizing her cards and creating systems to remember to write to people to thank them for different things. She sent several cards out in the mail every week, and that is a family practice I have kept going myself. I will send someone a thank-you note for just about anything. In fact, whenever I *receive* a thank-you note for something I did, I feel a little pull in my gut to send a thank-you note for their thank-you note!

Getting in the habit of writing thank-you notes forces us to slow down and actually notice the things that we are grateful for around us. I would like to think that ingratitude doesn't happen because most people are selfish or self-centered; I think we are all just too busy. We are always rushing from one thing to the next. When we have an unexpected blessing or act of kindness enter our lives, we appreciate it, but then we move directly on to the next thing on our to-do list for the day. By the time we get home at night and finally take a breath, that blessing is several hours and many activities behind us. We would absolutely make an effort to express gratitude or say a simple thank-you if we remembered to, but the fact is, most of the time we've already moved on. We just don't think about it because we're moving too fast.

We need to seriously ask ourselves, *Do I slow down long enough to recognize and express gratitude for the people, blessings, and acts of kindness in my life?* A commitment to writing thank-you notes, or maybe even writing a certain number of thank-you notes every week, helps us stay focused on that.

When I think of expressing gratitude, I am often reminded of the ten lepers Jesus healed in the seventeenth chapter of the Gospel of Luke. It was such a quick exchange, but it speaks volumes about our occasional inconsistency in expressing thanks. After the ten men ran off to present themselves to the priests as Jesus had instructed, only one returned to Him to express his sincere thanks for the miracle Jesus had just performed. You can almost feel the disappointment in Jesus's voice as He asks, "Didn't I heal ten men? Where are the other nine? Has no on returned to give glory to God except this foreigner?" (Luke 17:17–18, NLT).

Maybe the others were so excited that they ran home to tell their families the good news. Maybe they were so over-joyed by the life-changing miracle that they couldn't think straight. Or maybe they just took the miracle for granted. There's no way to know. Regardless, I never want to be one of "the other nine." We should always strive to be the one who returns to express gratitude in response to blessing. We cannot allow our busyness or excitement to lead us into what we might call "accidental ingratitude."

Send a Quick Text of Thanks

Now, while I'm a lifelong lover of handwritten thank-you notes, I will admit that I don't *only* use actual pen-and-paper notes when I want to send a word of thanks. Since the advent of smartphones, I've had a camera in my bag or pocket practically 24/7. And that camera has the ability to send quick, short messages to anyone anywhere in the world. That's a formerly unthinkable blessing itself, but the real value comes in using this miraculous device as an instrument of gratitude.

I love how easy cell phones have made the act of expressing thanks. Wherever I am, I have a good camera and the ability to send a quick note to someone. This is a great way to counter the "accidental ingratitude" caused by busyness. For example, I will often receive a card or thank-you note in the mail. That note shows me that someone was not only thinking of me but took the time to pray for me and write out a message of love or appreciation, stick that message in an envelope, write out my address, put a stamp on it, and drop it in the mailbox. We can take these cards for granted, but every card reflects a great deal of time and love. I joked earlier about sending a thank-you note for someone's thank-you note, but the truth is, I *do* send them a quick note of thanks. I just change the format.

Instead of writing out another actual card, I snap a picture of their card and attach it to a quick text to the person, saying something like, "I was so delighted to find this in the mailbox. It means so much to me that you took time out of your day to pray for me and think of me. Thank you so much." I can do that in about thirty seconds, and I probably send two or three of these texts every day.

Open Christmas and Birthday Cards Intentionally

This is a long-standing tradition whose days might be numbered, but I still love receiving Christmas cards (and birthday cards) in the mail. Like a thank-you note, these show that someone was thinking of me and went to some trouble to wish me a Merry Christmas. This is another act of love that we should be grateful for, but how often do we take these things for granted?

For years, John and I did what everybody else does when we received Christmas cards: we would take them out of the mailbox, pull the card out of the envelope, look at it for about five seconds, and then add the card to our growing collage of other Christmas cards we had received.

In the past few years, though, we've tried to be much more intentional about how we receive and process these holiday greetings. Rather than tearing into the envelope right away, we now put these incoming Christmas cards in a small stack on our coffee table. Then, every night throughout the holiday season, we take five cards off of the stack and sit down with them in our living room. We open one card together, read the greeting and look at the pictures, and then spend several minutes talking about that person or family and what they mean to us. We spend a few minutes praying for them, and then we send them a quick text or email thanking them for their card and telling them that we had prayed for them that night. Then, we move on to a second card. We do this for all five cards, and we do it almost every night throughout the holidays (and even well into the New Year until we're finished with the stack). It has become a wonderful new tradition for us. Not only is it a lovely way for us to spend time together, but it is a way to build in a new layer of gratitude into our busy lives.

Don't Give Them Everything They Want

The greatest thing my parents ever did for me related to gratitude was not giving me everything I asked for. We appreciate things more when we have to work for them, we must wait for them, or if we don't already have a house full of previous "wants." It creates an attitude of gratitude when you don't get everything you ask for or when you have to put some sweat and patience into it first—and children need to learn this lesson early and often.

I remember a girl I grew up with who always seemed to get everything she wanted. She lacked for nothing. Her parents simply bought her whatever she asked for. Now, what kind of life do you think this woman had once she got out from under her doting parents' roof? I'm afraid she has had nothing but difficulty throughout her entire adult life. She has been unsatisfied in her marriage, unsatisfied with her children's accomplishments, unsatisfied with the size and location of her home, unsatisfied with the cars she's had, unsatisfied with her income, and generally unsatisfied with life.

Why? I think it is because her parents set an unrealistic expectation for her that she could always simply have anything she wanted. If you learn that as a child, you are in for a rude awakening when you become an adult and are responsible for paying your own bills. It won't feel natural to wait or to save up for things. You won't understand why you can't have everything you want right now, because that's all you've ever known.

My father's business was doing quite well by the time I was a teenager. However, my parents never felt the need to upgrade their home, cars, clothes, or general lifestyle because they were making more money. Likewise, they felt no pressure to make sure my brothers and I had everything we wanted. They were more concerned with our character than our possessions. Sure, that was frustrating at times, but it has become the thing I am probably most grateful for in how they raised me.

I'm sure there are many things my parents would have enjoyed for themselves yet never purchased. They both lived in the same comfortable, humble, 1950s farmhouse that I had grown up in for the rest of their lives. My mother was certainly aware that most of the people who worked for my father lived in bigger and more extravagant homes, but she never really dealt with "house fever." In fact, she had to be talked into the handful of renovations they did do on the house. Just a few years before her death, we tried to get her to update her guest bathroom, which still had the original tiles from the 1950s. She wouldn't have any of it. She said, "There's nothing wrong with that bathroom. Everything still works, and it looks just like I wanted it to look when we did it the first time. Why would I change it?"

A big part of our modern culture of consumption is the never-ending list of things we want to get. As soon as we buy one thing, we start focusing on the next thing. And then the next, and then the next, and so on. But what if we tried to be *more grateful* for *fewer things* instead of just attaining more things we don't seem very grateful for? Which sounds better: to feel an enormous amount of satisfaction and gratitude for a few things or to feel very little satisfaction and gratitude for many things?

Most people go through life with this false idea that the more stuff you have, the better your life will be. That is usually not the case. I think the true secret to satisfaction is to focus more on appreciating and being grateful for the few things you do have than on the endless pursuit of more "stuff."

GOD IS SO, SO GOOD

John and I host a three-day camp experience for our grandchildren every summer (which I'll discuss more later). This past year, our camp theme was "So, So Good." All our activities and Bible lessons were built on the theme of the goodness of God. We wanted to stress to the children that God's blessings are always good, even when they don't "feel" particularly good at the time. We have several grandchildren who are quite young, so at first, we weren't entirely sure how to get the point of this message across. But then inspiration struck.

We brought the children into the kitchen one afternoon, where we had already set up a mock baking show with different bowls, utensils, and ingredients lying on the counter. We had prepared little chef hats for each of them to get them in the spirit of the activity. Then, we told them we were going to do a special "tasting." We lined the children up and presented them with several different surprise taste tests. We ran them through the gamut of milk, cocoa powder, chocolate chips, walnuts, buttermilk, lemons, sour cream, vanilla extract, and a few other things that might go into a dessert recipe. You can imagine that some of these items, like the chocolate chips, went over quite well. What child doesn't like a mouthful of chocolate? Other items, however, did not get such a positive response. Watching a five-year-old take a big sip of buttermilk is a sight you won't soon forget!

When the tasting was over, I explained to the children that God's blessings are often just like all those different ingredients they had just sampled. Some are sweet, and we think we can't get enough. Others are bitter, and we hope we never have to "taste" them again. Some may be salty, dry, bland, or creamy. Some may come in abundance, while others come only in tiny droplets. Taken as they come, we may not like some of the things God brings our way. But what happens when we put these ingredients together in one big mixing bowl? Dry cocoa, bitter buttermilk, and raw eggs can magically transform into the most delicious chocolate cake you could imagine! Each of those "gross" ingredients you *thought* you hated somehow works together to create something unexpectedly wonderful.

The same is true with all the different things God brings into our lives. Some of the blessings are fun and joyous. Some are bitter and painful. But what does God do? He mixes all these things together to create a rich, full, blessed life. He knows the good and the bad, and He knows how to use every single resource for the good of those who love Him (Romans 8:28). With the aftertaste of their taste test still in their mouths, we had the children read Psalm 34:8, "*Taste* and see that the LORD is good. Oh, the joys of those who take refuge in him!" (NLT, emphasis added).

Our tagline for camp that summer became a refrain we still often quote around our house: "When life is crazy, you'll hear me say that God is so, so good—better than the best thing." That's so true. When tragedy strikes . . . when your spouse gets a cancer diagnosis . . . when your beautiful grandson enters into eternity before ever drawing a breath on earth . . . you'll hear me say that God is so, so good—better than the best thing.

No, it's not always easy to say this. And no, it's not always easy to *mean* this. But God's blessings are abundant, and those blessings are often not what we ask for. Sometimes, they're the furthest thing from it. Yet the family value of gratitude provides a lens through which to see *all* the unexpected blessings of God…including those we can't immediately recognize.

CHAPTER 8

THE POWER OF "VALUE EXPERIENCES"

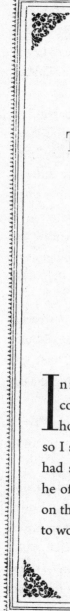I n my late teens, not long before I moved off to college, something got my dad thinking about how he'd done as a father. I was the youngest, so I suppose the prospect of me leaving home had stirred something unexpected in him. As he often told crowds of people when speaking on the topic of family and parenting, he started to wonder, "How have I done as a father? What

have I done well? What have I given Trudy? What trips and special things have meant the most to her?" The question that was *really* on his mind, though, which he probably didn't even realize at the time, was, "What will Trudy remember about me when I'm gone?"

That is a huge question—one I'm sure every parent has thought about, especially as their children prepare to leave the nest. My guess is that this question had probably been bothering my dad for a little while before he finally came to me and asked, "Trudy, what will you always remember that I did for you when you were growing up?"

I said, "Dad, I think I'm always going to remember the times you would come home late from work after I'd gone to bed, check to see if my lights were still on, and if they were, come into my room to talk to me."

It would be late. I knew he was tired. He was still wearing his work clothes. He smelled like chicken (as always). But if he saw my bedroom light on at the end of the hall, he would sometimes use whatever energy he had left over from the day to come talk to me.

He would sit down on my bed next to me and say, "Trudy, do you want to tell me about your day?" That was the most treasured time that I had with my dad.

My answer to his question genuinely surprised him. He said, "Wow, I wish I had done that more often. I don't even recall doing that very much." It was not something that was very memorable or remarkable to my dad, but it was significant to me. It was an *experience,* an investment he made in my life, using his time and energy to engage with me in a unique and personal way. And it definitely left a mark on my life.

Today, like my father, I often speak on the topic of family and parenting. In those talks, I often ask people, "Who were the influencers in your life? Tell me a little something about them and why they were so influential to you." Their responses are remarkably consistent. People tell me about a coach, a teacher, a grandparent, a Sunday school teacher, or some other mentor-type figure. Maybe it was a coach who encouraged them to do their best or a teacher who noticed they were really good at something and encouraged them in that area. Maybe it was a spiritual mentor who modeled a life of faith like no one else ever had.

Interestingly, nobody ever answers that question by telling me about something someone purchased for them. They never tell me about birthday presents or Christmas presents, and it's even pretty rare for someone to tell me about some extravagant vacation or other huge expense. Instead, I consistently hear about small, everyday interactions that cost nothing but someone's time and intentionality.

Too often, we get this idea in our head that, in order to impact someone's life, we have to spend a lot of money or do a lot of things for them. In reality, though, it is often the smallest things that have the biggest impact. Because of this, I'm a strong advocate for investing in *experiences* more than in *things*. This is something John and I have been extremely intentional about, first as parents, but now even more so as grandparents. We understand that the best way to preserve and transfer the values that make us who we are as a family is not through lectures or extravagant spending, and it certainly isn't through sitting idly by, crossing our fingers, and *hoping* our children and grandchildren see what we want them to see in our lives. No, the best way to make sure our family values are picked up and carried forward by the next generation is to wrap those values in meaningful "value experiences" that our children and grandchildren can engage in and keep alive in their hearts.

But what exactly is a value experience, and what makes it so powerful?

EXPERIENCES MAKE MEMORIES LAST FOREVER

Experiences provide what you might call *emotional longevity*. They take up space in our hearts and minds in a way that physical things—*stuff*—can't. They plant a flag in our memories. They become important markers on the journey. Simply put, they *last*.

Things break. We outgrow them, we lose them, we don't like them anymore. But experiences stay with us, even while an endless stream of "things" come and go.

Things may knock around our rooms, closets, garages, and attics for decades, but their *value* doesn't endure. Instead, the emotional value of things starts depreciating almost as soon as we get them. By the time we throw them out (like last year's must-have Christmas gift), there's barely any meaning left. Experiences, in contrast, are just the opposite: they have a short lifespan, in that the experience itself may last only an hour, a day, or at best a week, but the experience has an *appreciating* value. It can start becoming more meaningful and taking up more space in your heart and mind the further you get away from it. An experience is generally a small investment of time, effort, and intentionality, but it will pay enormous emotional, spiritual, and relational dividends over the long haul.

Experiences Freeze a Moment in Time

Every parent and grandparent knows that time moves way, way too fast. We have a sense of this when we're younger, before we have children, but once we have a child, the passage of times becomes frighteningly real. We're no longer marking time by the wrinkles that slowly appear on our faces or the weight gain that creeps up on us over the course of many years. Instead, we see our baby become a toddler seemingly overnight. And then we see that toddler learning to drive a car. And then we see that car driving off, taking our no-longer-a-baby away to start a family of his or her own. Where does the time go?

We've been blessed with sixteen grandchildren. The younger ones are still toddling around, but the older ones are close to graduating high school. How did the time fly by so quickly?

Usually, when we're in the day-to-day grind of raising our children, a day can feel like an eternity. It has been more than forty years, but I still remember being at home with our children when they were very, very young. Some days move like molasses, don't they? I remember so many times watching the clock and counting down the hours until John got home from work or travel just so I could have a moment or two for myself. But at the same time, we would reach the end of the year or a child's birthday, and I would think, *How in the world are we already here again?* It is like my mother used to say, "Days are long, but life is short."

At least once a week, I'll get a reminder on social media showing me a picture of something that happened one year ago, three years ago, five years ago, ten years ago. I will look at those memories and think, *Wow, so much time has passed. I can't believe this was five years ago. I am so glad I took time to do (whatever we were doing in the picture) with the grandchildren!* It might be a picture of a holiday or a vacation. What is so interesting is that the children might not even remember any of the details about the trip or the gift. But they *do* remember spending time with me. They remember conversations we had on that trip, jokes we told, games we played, and funny things that happened. They remember the *experience*. And, God willing, they always will.

For example, just last night as I sit here writing this, I was invited to my grandson Michael's eleventh birthday dinner. My daughter Angela and her husband were taking Michael out with his other grandparents. John happened to be out of town, so I had been home alone for a few nights and Angela thought it would be fun for me to get out of the house.

At first, I said no. It is important for Michael's other grandparents to spend time with him on his actual birthday, and I did not want to get in their way or intrude on their time at all. However, my daughter insisted they wouldn't mind and really encouraged me to go.

The handful of times a year that John is away, I generally try to maximize my time. I go into deep work mode and knock out a lot of tasks. So, my to-do list included preparing to write this chapter, revising previous chapters, preparing for an upcoming talk I'm giving, and other important tasks when this unexpected invitation came in. As I thought more about it, however, I realized I was being invited into a very special experience for Michael. It was his birthday—the only eleventh birthday dinner he would ever have—and he wanted me to be there. Knowing that "life is short," I realized I should go. Time is going to fly by, so I'd better take advantage of every opportunity I have.

We Pay a Price for Missed Opportunities

If each experience with your loved ones has so much potential, long-lasting value, then the flip side is also true: we pay a potentially enormous price for *missed* opportunities. How many times have you decided not to join a group of friends for a night or weekend away, only to discover later that it was the best night of their lives? That missed opportunity can feel like a hole in our lives. We can only dream about what the experience *might* have meant to us, and we feel a void whereas others who participated in the experience feel newly filled. And sometimes that void can sit in your spirit for the rest of your life.

My mother was raised by a single mother in the 1920s and 1930s. Her mother, whom we always called Granny, was a remarkable and strong woman. She was also pretty much the only family member on my mother's side who we ever saw. She was an important part of our family, and I loved her very much.

Granny passed away while John and I were serving in Brazil. It was a difficult time for my mother, losing her own mother while her only daughter was out of the country. Yet, for some reason I'll never fully understand, my mother did not let us know for more than a week that Granny had died. In fact, I did not find out until after the funeral service. My mother knew I would feel a deep responsibility to be there for her, so I suppose she thought she was saving me the trouble of flying home for a week or two. Instead, that decision left the sting of a missed opportunity that I still feel just as deeply to this day, more than thirty years later.

I really wish she had called me as soon as Granny took a turn for the worse. It would have meant so much to me to be there to support my mother through that experience. With me out of the country, Mom relied on my father and two brothers for emotional support. But I really feel she and I could have had a beautiful experience sharing that grief woman-to-woman.

That was an important experience I missed, and I truly believe its absence has left a small hole in my life. I feel that loss every time I think about my grandmother.

It's so easy to think about how much experiences mean to our lives, but we always need to be on the lookout for opportunities for meaningful experiences that we're in danger of missing out on. While I absolutely believe there is tremendous value in saying no to things in order to protect your time, we can't get so used to saying no that we turn our backs on the experiences that can truly shape our lives.

An Experience Is a Memory Multiplier

Experiences linger long after the event happens. A fun, meaningful experience gives us true joy—not just in the moment but for a long time afterward. I like to say that an experience is a *memory multiplier*. The further you get from that experience, the more joy you might feel going back there in your mind and telling that story. That's what I meant earlier when I said experiences have an *appreciating value*. Like any good investment, they become even more valuable over time.

Think about some of your favorite family stories, the ones that are always told around the Thanksgiving table or at family reunions. Isn't it interesting that the experience of simply telling the story becomes an experience in and of itself? One experience from years past is literally creating another one today! That's when you know your memories have been multiplied. The joy you felt on the day of the experience just keeps growing and growing every time you think about it or tell the story.

The Best Gift You Can Give Your Children and Grandchildren

I mentioned my grandson's eleventh birthday earlier. I gave Michael a Lego set for his birthday, and he was very excited to get it. However, in ten years, there's almost no chance he'll be able to remember what I got him for his eleventh birthday. But hopefully, he will remember me being at his birthday dinner. Maybe it will just be a flash in his mind, or maybe he'll look back at some pictures we took that night and will see me there laughing and smiling and celebrating with him. Even if he cannot recall the conversation we had, and even if he doesn't remember that night at all in his conscious mind, I know my being there at the very least added one more brick to the relationship he and I will continue to build.

I am perfectly happy with the twenty or thirty dollars I spent on Legos for him, but I am much happier about the two hours I invested into our relationship that night.

Speaking of birthdays, mine is at what many consider the worst possible time for a birthday: the week before Christmas. Those of us with December birthdays know that it can be easy for your birthday to get lost amid all the holiday bustle. However, my mother always tried to make sure I had a birthday party. She never wanted me to feel like my birthday didn't matter even though it was so close to Christmas. For several years in a row, my friends Gayla and Terri came over for a special birthday sleepover. We had so much fun together. My mother loved it when we got dressed up in costumes, stood in front of the fireplace, and put on a little show to entertain my parents. I loved it too.

Out of all the birthdays I spent in that house, I can remember only one birthday present my parents gave me—but I remember those birthday sleepovers. I remember performing in my living room with my friends, blowing out candles while everyone sang to me, eating cake, and having fun with my family and friends. Again, the time and money we spend on creating experiences with our family is an investment that will pay huge dividends in the long run.

PRESERVE AND TRANSFER VALUES THROUGH EXPERIENCES

Why all the fuss about creating meaningful experiences after we've spent so many chapters discussing the importance of defining your unique set of family values? Simple: because the best way by far to *preserve* those values throughout your lifetime and *transfer* them to the next generation is to wrap them in unforgettable experiences that you share with your children and grandchildren. Children will forget most of what you *tell* them and half of what you *show* them; their memories will form and harden around what you *do with them*.

Therefore, I want to challenge you to create a set of specific, intentional experiences based on your family values that are designed to be memorable, keystone events in your child or grandchild's life. I will take some time here to describe the six experiences we've developed that work very well for us, but this doesn't mean you have to do exactly what we're doing. In fact, you shouldn't! Your value experiences should be tailor-made just for your family, taking all your own unique factors into account. We'll talk about how to bring these events together in the following chapter. For now, let me describe what works for us.

Experience 1: Birthday Trips for the Grandchildren

As our older grandchildren approached age eight, John and I started talking about ways we could carve out special one-on-one time with each of them in a meaningful way. We loved spending time with everyone as a family group, but we also wanted to delve deeper into our relationships with each individual child. We wanted our "grands" to know their Mimi and Papa, to really *get to know us,* just as we wanted to have more intimate relationships with each of them. We had a strong desire to build unique and fun memories with them on an individual level, beyond the context of the entire family. So, we started talking about ways to make that happen.

Ultimately, we decided to make a commitment to take each grandchild on a special trip—just the three of us—to celebrate their birthday. Of course, with so many grandchildren, we're celebrating one or two birthdays a month on average as it is, so we knew it would be impossible to take them each out for *every* birthday. We narrowed it down, talked to their parents, and decided that we would take our grandchildren on a special birthday trip four times—for their eighth, eleventh, fourteenth, and seventeenth birthdays. We figured that would give us plenty of one-on-one time with them at different stages of their young lives.

We do our best to plan each trip especially for that particular child, using their interests and hobbies as a guide. And, of course, we aren't talking about weeklong jungle safaris or nonstop trips to Disney World. Instead, these are usually just long weekends away, maybe to the beach or to a mountain cabin. One of our granddaughters loves dancing, so we took her to New York for a Broadway show. Several grandsons enjoy sports, so we've traveled to see a ball game here and there. We've also taken trips to Nashville to enjoy the music; Washington, DC, to take in the political sites; Boston to visit the historical landmarks; and more.

The oldest, Ashlynn, recently turned seventeen, and we chose Disney World, spending a few days with her taking in some shows, riding a few rides, eating at some specialty restaurants, and doing more grown-up activities with her there. We had a wonderful time, but all three of us seemed aware of the fact that this was our last scheduled trip with her. I still can't believe she's already seventeen!

I want to be clear that these trips don't have to be big, expensive, blowout experiences. In fact, it's best that they aren't. We prefer simple moments with plenty of time to talk and enjoy being together. If you want to try this with your children or grandchildren, remember that you don't even have to leave town. You could plan a special "staycation" for the child, having them stay at your house and simply take day trips to nearby parks, ball games, amusement parks, and so on. The point isn't to try and impress them with an extravagant trip; the point is to spend quality time with each child as an individual.

These trips have given John and me several opportunities to live out our family values in front of the grandchildren. We let the children see us live out our faith, love on our family, act and speak with integrity, give generously, and express gratitude. We talk to them about these things and (hopefully) provide a good example for what these values can and should look like in practice.

When these children grow up and look back on their time with us, I want them to remember their grandparents as individuals, not just as a family fixture. That's why we've invested so much time and trouble into creating these special birthday experiences for them. I can only pray we have enough time left to take the last grandchild on his seventeenth birthday trip!

Experience 2: Family Vacation

Every year, all five of our families (John and me and our four children's families) take a weeklong vacation together right after Christmas. We kick it off with our family Christmas Eve tradition (although it's usually not actually on Christmas Eve) of sitting around the Christmas tree as one big family wearing matching Christmas pajamas and enjoying all twenty-five of us being together as one big group. The adults usually enjoy sitting and talking around the fire while all the cousins scatter all over the house, having a good time playing together. Everyone stays at our house that night, with cousins sharing bedrooms, which adds to the fun. And then, we'll get up the next morning and head off for our annual family vacation.

This trip really spotlights our family, generosity, and gratitude values. Obviously, being together as a family—often under the same roof for a week—hits the family value. We bring the generosity and gratitude values in by spending some trips doing some mission and service work together wherever we are. I wouldn't necessarily call this a mission trip per se, but there's definitely mission work to be done during this week.

Obviously, these trips can get expensive, and I know it isn't something everyone can do. And I understand that the prospect of spending an entire week with the whole family together can be intimidating to many grandparents, parents, and children. However, even if you can't (or don't want to) spend an entire week away with the whole family, I challenge you to think of things you *can* do together. Maybe you could spend one night under the same roof and then get up the next day to do a service project together. Again, this isn't about having a fancy, expensive vacation; it's about spending time together as a family doing something in line with your family values. These annual trips work great for us; what could you do with your family to bring everyone together around one of your key values?

Experience 3: Family Reunion

My parents loved going to the beach. As I've said before, despite Dad's remarkable success in business, he and Mom remained "simple folks" until their dying day. When it came to travel, while they enjoyed a few special trips over the years, their favorite place to get away was their condo in Florida. As they got older, my brothers and I tried to get them to take in some new experiences, but we always ended up back at the beach. There was one trip in particular that sealed the deal. The entire Cathy family—Mom and Dad, my two brothers and their families, and my family—had planned a fun ski trip to Colorado. However, as soon as we landed, Mom's health took a nosedive. The change in altitude had a negative impact on her blood pressure, and we realized we couldn't even take her up the mountain to the resort. She stayed at the foot of the mountain for a while to get acclimated and then eventually made it up the mountain to our hotel. After that episode, though, my parents' vacation mindset was "Beach or bust!"

Those beach trips became cherished time for our extended family. My brothers and I were very close growing up on the farm together, but the twenty-plus years I spent in Alabama, Brazil, and Virginia meant we grew up separated by hundreds or thousands of miles from our extended family. Bringing everyone together for several days, though logistically difficult, was a huge blessing. After our parents passed away, Dan, Bubba, and I knew that it was up to us to continue preserving our family tradition of getting the family together. One way we did this was to maintain our annual beach trips, which we came to view as our "Cathy Family Retreat." Once a year, more than sixty of us descend on the beach to relax, play, share meals, and tell old stories. Everyone comes when and for as long as they can, so people are always coming and going. It is such a wonderful time to see the whole family together.

I'm afraid the whole concept of the family reunion seems a bit old-fashioned these days. We simply don't hear about them as much as we used to. That's a shame. Families need to spend time together, and that includes extended families representing several generations. Being together as one large family reminds you and teaches the children that they were not born in isolation. They are part of a family, and that family has shared values and shared experiences. That family has an *identity*, like we discussed earlier in the book.

Looking around and seeing the different faces of grandparents, aunts, uncles, nieces, nephews, and cousins reminds us that we are *connected* to these people. We may not always agree. We may not enjoy the same things. But we are connected as a family. We share a name, genetic traits, physical similarities, cultural backgrounds, ancestors, and perhaps most importantly, shared family stories.

My favorite part of our family retreat is simply listening to everybody talk about funny and meaningful things that happened in the past. Everywhere you look, groups of family members are chatting away, telling stories about the family, sharing what they remember and who did what. You hear the older family members talk about what they did before you were born. You learn about your grandparents' grandparents, what life was like back then, and why your family does things a certain way or believes certain things. You look at picture albums, taking note of who in previous generations had your eyes or your nose or your smile. You acknowledge and appreciate the family foundation you all share.

I know it can be difficult planning a reunion for the family and getting a good response from everyone, but these don't have to be gigantic, destination vacation reunions. It's not about where you go; it's about what you do—and the fact that you're doing it together. Our extended family enjoys having reunions at the beach, but you can be as creative as you want with the location. You can have just as meaningful of an experience renting out a local banquet hall, sharing a meal in the church fellowship hall, or gathering at the park pavilion for an afternoon. Whatever you choose and wherever you go, the key value here is in spending time with the family engaging in shared activities, doing things together, and creating new memories and new stories to share later.

Experience 4: Annual Family Assembly

Once our children were grown, John and I knew we needed to shift our thinking about them a bit. Whereas we'd spent twenty years or so seeing them as children, we needed to start thinking of them as who they had become: adults. We were certainly proud of the men and women they'd become, and we know this is where many parents think they're "done" parenting. But we wanted to stay involved and help guide and mentor them through their adult years too—albeit in a much different way than we did when they were young. After discussing this for a while, John and I came up with the idea of bringing our children together for what we have come to call our Family Assembly. This is a weekend retreat in the mountains that we take with our adult children and their spouses. I mentioned this assembly in chapter 2; this was when and where we led our children through the values exercise one year (and where they called us out for not having written out our own values).

We treat this assembly like an annual family business retreat. This is our dedicated time to discuss careers, updates on Chick-fil-A (especially helpful for those who aren't involved day-to-day in the company), family business, and estate planning. We also spend a good bit of time talking about the giving we do as a family, and John and I dig into the causes our children are giving to, which often introduces us to wonderful new causes and opportunities to bless people. We might also do a book study together, and of course we spend time in prayer for each other, lifting each individual's needs up to the Lord.

The agenda is a bit different every year, but our values are almost always represented in our discussions and the time we spend together as a family of adults away from their children. The ten of us have gotten incredibly close through this assembly, and

I look forward to it every year. It's been a remarkable blessing to have these opportunities to see the godly, intelligent, fun, wonderful men and women God has made them all to be.

Experience 5: Assembly for Grands

Our Family Assembly has been so effective at equipping our adult children in their work, marriages, finances, and more that John and I began discussing a way in which we might provide a similar experience for our grandchildren—the next generation of our family-owned business. I was practically raised in the kitchen of my father's restaurant, my children grew up hearing about the business and its people, and some of the third generation are already working in different roles in the company. We recognize not every grandchild will go into the business, of course, but they'll all be touched by it. As such, we want to help prepare them for what it might look like to be a Company Ambassador.

After talking it over with our adult children, John and I decided to start a new annual assembly—one specifically for our grandchildren age thirteen and up. Like the older version, this is framed as a weekend retreat, but we mix in a little more fun here than we do with their parents. We might go out for a picnic or go boating, for instance, but we also spend plenty of time inside the cabin doing little workshops. This is our time to teach our grandchildren about our family values; help them learn how to identify their own personal values, purpose, and strengths; give lessons on simple budgeting and basic business practices; and play engaging games about "who's who" among the Chick-fil-A family.

Our goal with this Assembly for Grands is to help prepare each grandchild to do whatever God calls them to do in life, whether it is business, medicine, parenting, or anything else. Whatever they do and wherever they go, they will all be "ambassadors" representing the family. We want them to be confident young men and women who know how to make good decisions, and we want to help launch them into society to make a difference for the kingdom.

Experience 6: Camp MiPa

Our sixth and last regular values experience is Camp MiPa, our annual camp experience for all our grandchildren (or at least the ones who are out of diapers). This is where I draw on my thirteen years as a Camp Director and lead the children through several days of camp-inspired activities in our home and around the farm. Their parents have to register them online just like they would with a "real" camp, and everyone is divided up and assigned different "cabins," or bedrooms around our house. We spend a few days doing Bible studies, playing games, camping, cooking, and everything else you'd expect from a summer camp. This has become a staple of the children's childhood and has given us all so many wonderful memories together. Plus, it has given the four sets of cousins an unusual amount of time together—time they've spent bonding as family and, more importantly, as friends. It's an amazing thing to watch the children you love so much love each other so well!

COMMEMORATING THE EXPERIENCES

After these experiences are over—whether it's one of our six planned value experiences, a holiday, or any other special event—I try to take some time to create a keepsake to commemorate the experience. The best tool I have for that is a custom photobook, which is super easy to create and fairly inexpensive to buy from many online photo service companies. This is such a powerful way to commemorate the experience and create a physical memory that you can use later for telling stories or looking back on your time together.

I realize that taking pictures is commonplace these days, but we've gotten in the habit of posting photos to social media and then forgetting about them. When I was a little girl, it was a big deal to gather around the family photo albums because photos were much rarer in those days. Today, though, it's not uncommon for people to take more than a hundred photos every single day! That's great, but what do you do with all those pictures? Sometimes it seems like the more pictures we take, the less we actually look at them. Taking the pictures out of the digital world and bringing them into the physical world with a book that you can sit down with and flip through together—or that you can see on your coffee table and instantly be taken back mentally and emotionally to a special time you shared with your loved ones—adds a whole new dimension to the entire experience.

FIND WHAT WORKS FOR YOUR FAMILY

I feel like I should say this one more time: the experiences I've described in this chapter represent what works for *our* family, not yours. Just as I said when I shared my family's five values, I'm only giving you these as an *example of what you might do*. These are *our* experiences; they work very well for us in our situation and considering our values. Your family will likely be much different and therefore have different needs, resources, considerations, and opportunities. Every family will approach this from a different starting point based on their values, faith system, budget, available time, geographic proximity to family members, and, of course, how close they are as a family unit. As such, there is no *one way* or *one experience* that is "right" for every family. You'll have to take the examples I provided here and the instructions I'll provide in the next chapter and figure out what works for you. The experiences you come up with may be similar to ours, or they may be a million miles apart. That's okay! In fact, that's great! That means your family value experiences will be *your* experiences—and that's exactly what we want to create.

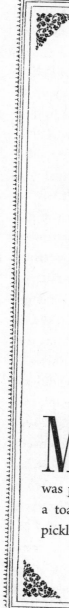
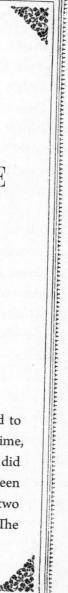

CHAPTER 9

HOW TO CREATE
PERSONALIZED VALUE
EXPERIENCES

My father was a simple man. He used to make jokes about himself all the time, playing up the fact that all he ever did was put a boneless breast of chicken between a toasted buttered hamburger bun with two pickles and called it a chicken sandwich. The truth is, though, he was brilliant in several areas. Perhaps the biggest one was his ability to create excellent experiences for people.

From the day he opened his first business—at literally eight years old—he was laser-focused on working with the highest degree of excellence possible. Even as a boy, he modeled the biblical ideal of work: "Work willingly at whatever you do, as though you were working for the Lord rather than for people. Remember that the Lord will give you an inheritance as your reward, and that the Master you are serving is Christ" (Colossians 3:23–24, NLT). People may look at the success Chick-fil-A enjoys today and imagine my father starting off already a wealthy, successful entrepreneur. That's not how it happened at all. My father grew up in very humble circumstances. He often described himself as a simple boy with a simple mind who didn't have a lot. What he did have, though, was this incredible drive to do everything with excellence and to give the highest level of service possible.

In 1929, at eight years old, he started selling bottles of Coca-Cola on the street. He quickly realized that people were more likely to enjoy (and therefore purchase) his Cokes if they weren't warm, so he always made sure to keep them cold. This was a bit harder back then than it is today. In those days, ice was delivered to your home in one big block, which his mother kept in the icebox. He liked to say that he "borrowed" enough ice out of his mom's icebox to keep his Cokes cold long enough to sell them. Sometimes, when the delivery man dropped off his family's ice for the week, he asked the delivery person if there were any smaller pieces that had broken off his other deliveries that he could keep. He collected all the extra ice he could to keep his wagon full of Cokes cold.

At age eleven, he got a paper route. But he wasn't content to just throw the papers in the yard. He got to know each customer on his route and learned where each person preferred to have their paper dropped off. Then, he did his best to hit that exact spot for each house he delivered to. That's obviously unusual for a paper boy, and word started to get out that this Cathy boy provided excellent service. As I've shared earlier in this book, "A good name is more desirable than great riches" (Proverbs 22:1, NIV). That commitment to excellence—to creating a unique, memorable, and enjoyable experience for every customer—is still the heart of Chick-fil-A today. Of all the awards we have won and continue to win, the one we are proudest of is our consistent number one ranking in the industry's leading customer satisfaction polls. We see that as our customers' recognition of the effort we put into creating an excellent experience for them.

As I was preparing to write this chapter, I couldn't help but think of my father's commitment to creating excellent experiences for every single customer. And then I began to wonder, *How does this happen in the home?* That is, what can we do to make sure our children are going to remember the important things we talked about while they were in the home? How can we provide them with experiences that are so unique, meaningful, and downright excellent that the values we are trying to communicate become firmly rooted in their hearts and minds?

With few exceptions, I truly believe every parent wants to be the best parent they could possibly be. I've never known a parent who strived to be mediocre. But, as we've seen, success does not happen by accident. In the same way, you will not trip and fall into excellent experiences. It takes work, planning, and above all, intentionality.

SIX STEPS FOR CREATING MEMORABLE VALUE EXPERIENCES IN YOUR HOME

This chapter is your action plan. My goal here is to provide a clear playbook you can use to start implementing your own set of unique, custom-made value experiences designed to drive your family values deep into the hearts of your children and/or grandchildren. These are six simple steps that anyone should be able to implement on any budget—as long as you're willing to put in a little time and effort.

Step 1: Prepare Yourself

The first step is potentially the biggest, and that is to prepare yourself. You can't preserve and transfer your family values if you don't know what they are! That's why we spent so much time at the start of this book discussing the importance of values and the need to articulate the handful of values that represent who you are as a person and as a family. Here, I'm going to run through a handful of things you can do to prepare yourself to create memorable value experiences for your family, but some of these will just be quick reminders of items we've already covered.

Opening Questions

To start, I recommend spending time in prayer and reflection as you ask yourself the following questions. Don't just do this in your head, though. Grab a pen and notebook or open a new note on your phone or computer's notes app and write down some thoughtful responses. And, of course, if you're married, do this exercise with your spouse as you consider:

1. What really matters to me?
2. Who do we want our children to be when they leave our home?
3. What traits or values are most important to us and why?
4. How does God want to use our family to impact the kingdom, and what gifts has He given us personally to use in that mission?

These questions are designed to get your mind in the right place before you launch into the more time-consuming and tactical tasks.

Identify Your Top Three to Five Values

We spent an entire chapter early in this book discussing how and why you should identify the handful of values that best represent who you are as a family. If you have not yet completed this exercise, I strongly encourage you to stop now, go back to chapter 2, and use either the values cards or the values word bank to narrow down your top three to five values.

The process of identifying values will help you articulate your own calling and purpose in life. It will help
inform the actions and decisions you make, and it will help
create some traditions because it will allow you to focus
on what's important. The traditions we treasure are very
often a spin-off from our values. When something is so
important to you, you create traditions to exercise, transfer,
and preserve that value.

For example, old friends who live out of state might
prioritize getting together a few times a year. This could be
something like seasonal fishing or hunting trips, a tradition
of going to a certain sporting event together every year, an
annual mountain retreat or beach trip, and so on. While the
people involved enjoy the activities in these examples, the
real reason for the trip is to maintain, preserve, and honor a
longtime friendship. Some of these traditions have a limited
season in that they happen only for a while and then they stop.
Others will go on forever.

Values also help protect the margin in your life around
what is important. None of us can do *everything*. We each have
only a certain amount of time, and we each must decide how,
when, where, and on what we will invest that time. It is so easy
to fill up your entire life with things that are "good," but are
those things *really* good if they only pull you away from the
things that are most important to you? As the saying goes,
the enemy of great is not *bad*; the true enemy of great is *good*.
When we focus on things that are merely good, we often leave
little room for the things that are truly great.

Post Your Values Around Your House

Too often, individuals or businesses go through lengthy exercises to identify their purpose and values. But then they don't do anything with them. They leave their results on a sheet of paper or in a notebook and never look at them again. If you identify the things that truly matter to you, you cannot leave them on the shelf. These things deserve a place in your life. Remember, these should not be *new* things. You are simply identifying what is *already* important to you and your family. So, keep them in front of you.

In its most basic form, this could simply be writing your values on a Post-It Note and sticking it on your bathroom mirror so you see it when you wake up and when you get ready for bed every night. You could create a bookmark that lists your values to use in the books you are reading or in your Bible. You could stick a list of them on the dashboard of your car so you see them whenever you're driving around. You could make a custom wallpaper for your phone or computer with your values listed out. These don't have to be big posters or works of art. You are not doing this for anyone else; it is just for you. The only goal here is to see your values regularly, to interact with them, to be confronted daily with what you have identified as important in your life.

Adjust Your Life to Your Values

If these things truly represent what is important to you, ask yourself what changes you might need to make in your life to better reflect those values. By reflect I mean your values should be evident in your calendar, finances, commitments, opportunities of influence, behavior, reputation, and every other part of your life. Simply put, if you aren't actively *doing* the things you say you value, you've either misidentified your values or you are poorly prioritizing your resources.

Be Accountable to Someone

It is one thing to write your values down on a note card for yourself; it is quite another thing to let other people know about them. Being public about your values, and especially inviting a trusted friend or mentor to hold you accountable for them, introduces a whole new dimension of responsibility and accountability. Sharing your values with someone makes you "put some skin in the game," so to speak. It ups the ante, meaning you know there will be a price to pay if you fail to live out those values. That price could just be embarrassment or the disappointment of a mentor, but even that is a real motivator in our lives to stay true to who we say we want to be. If you never tell anyone your goals and values, it is so much easier to let yourself off the hook when you don't want to live them out.

Step 2: Focus on Improving the Experience

Wherever you are and whatever your role is, you must always be asking yourself, "How can I create the best experience possible?"

- At home, how can you do this for your family?
- If you are a teacher, how can you do this in the classroom?

- If you lead people, how can you do this with your team at work?

As I've said, my father had a wonderful instinct for this, even as a young boy. It's something I learned by watching him, and it's something I've tried to incorporate into all my roles, both personal and professional.

For example, when John and I originally discussed hosting all our grandchildren for a few days each summer, I knew it needed to be something more than the typical "visit at the grandparents' house." I didn't want all those grandchildren to be bored, and I didn't want to waste those precious days with them all under one roof. So, I asked that fundamental question, "How can I create the best experience possible?" I thought about how I'd done that in my role working with large groups of children as a Camp Director and realized I had the perfect opportunity to create a unique, meaningful, memorable experience for my grandchildren by simply doing what I had done professionally for thirteen years: lead them through a fun, structured summer camp experience! It was such an obvious answer—but it was obvious only because I had stopped to ask myself the question.

As you think through how you can improve the experience, start with the low-hanging fruit, the tools and experience already at your disposal. You might do what I did and think about how you could incorporate things you've learned at work. So often, we are masters of something professionally but never stop to think how we might bring that area of expertise into our family lives. That's like the world's greatest party planner failing to throw her own child a decent birthday party! What ultimate good is all the talent, skill, and experience you exercise at work if you can't use it to further the kingdom and bless your own family?

Another tip in improving the experience is to reject any notion of "settling." Don't settle for a *good* experience if you can push it just one or two steps further to make it a *great* experience for your family. Always ask yourself, "Is this the *best* I can do, or is this the *easiest* thing I can do? Is there just a little bit more I could do that could make an exponential impact on this experience?"

Step 3: Make the Experience Memorable

From his earliest days in business, my father understood that the customer wants a unique experience. If the experience is routine and expected, it is not going to be something they remember. As a result, Chick-fil-A has worked hard to create unique experiences with every customer, thereby creating *memorable* experiences. We take this very seriously in our hiring and training. That is why it is not at all uncommon to see social media posts about Chick-fil-A Team Members changing a customer's flat tire in the parking lot or having as many Team Members working *outside* in the drive-thru lanes as we do *inside* the restaurant. These things are not accidents. They are the direct result of our commitment to create truly memorable experiences.

For example, I work with the children's ministry at my church, and we have a different Bible study theme for the children every month. But we go far beyond simply teaching around a theme each month. To create these truly memorable experiences, we decorate the children's ministry area according to that month's theme, and we even make smaller tweaks to the decor from week to week. When the children walk into the room, they can't help but notice the differences, which then plays into the lessons we are teaching them that week. By doing this, we are trying to create some memorable moments for these children instead of just having the same old thing every Sunday when they come to church.

How can you do this at home? It can be as easy as randomly making a big deal out of something otherwise mundane. If your child has a big test one day, for instance, you could treat them to their favorite breakfast or stop for coffee on the way to school. My son-in-law Trent often does this for his daughter. They don't do it every day, but if he knows she's a little anxious about something or it's a big day, he'll be sure to leave early enough to run through a drive-thru somewhere to get some coffee or breakfast for her.

You might start leaving notes for your children around the house. You can leave notes of encouragement for your teenager on their bathroom mirror. If you make lunch for younger children, you could leave little notes in their lunch box. Or you could surprise your children with balloons and decorations on a random day just like you might do on their birthday.

If your child has a sporting event, you could go the extra mile by making big signs with their name on it for the game so that you can cheer them on from the stands. Because I work in my church's children's ministry, I generally hear about most of the children's sporting events. It's rare that I'm able to go, but I do when I can. I'm always surprised by how meaningful it is to a young child when someone—even a Sunday school teacher—goes out of their way to come to a sporting event just to cheer them on.

In all of this, the goal is to deliver well above their expectations. We do this so often at work, and many companies even have dedicated employees or whole departments focused on creating these kinds of memorable experiences for customers. The problem is, even people who do this professionally can fail to see the value of doing it at home.

In my book *A Quiet Strength*, I wrote about how my mother always stood at the back door whenever any of us left the house. She would stop whatever she was doing and walk with us to the door. There, she would say goodbye, tell us that she loved us, and almost without fail say, "And remember *who you are* and *whose you are!*"

This made such an impact on me that, to this day, if I fail to stop what I'm doing and intentionally say goodbye to my husband, children, or grandchildren when they leave my house, I feel a little tinge of guilt. As a teenager, I never appreciated how much effort my mom put into creating this experience for us. Once I became a wife and mother, though, it finally dawned on me how difficult it is to stop whatever I'm doing whenever someone walks out the door. It can feel like a constant stream of interruptions when you're trying to accomplish something around the house. I don't know how my mother managed to do it every single time—but I'm so glad she did. That consistent experience left a mark on me— one that will echo in my heart for the rest of my life.

I know full well how easy it is to get in a rut and let your creativity grow cold, especially as you grow older. John and I have definitely faced that in our own lives. That's why I'm trying to light a fire under you here. The things we're talking about in this book don't have to be huge, expensive, time-consuming events. You'd be shocked by how many powerful, lifelong memories can be forged with just a little bit of creativity, time, and intentionality.

Step 4: Prioritize Your Time

We've talked several times throughout this book about how experiences require an investment—sometimes financial but always in time and intentionality. And, like any resource, you have to prioritize how you are going to spend your time every day. Part of this prioritization should go to creating unique and memorable experiences.

However...

I want to be crystal clear here when I talk about *what* I think deserves priority in your family. I think every married couple with children has faced a kind of "priority crisis" when it comes to figuring out how and where to focus their time. If you're married, it can be so easy to prioritize your children above your spouse. Perhaps without even fully realizing it, we tell ourselves, "My number one job is to make my children feel loved and protected and to raise them well." That certainly sounds noble, but where does it leave your spouse? We lose sight of the fact that, in a marriage, God calls us *first* as a spouse and *then* as a parent. Even as a practical matter, your spouse was there before your children were born, and (ideally) he or she will be there after your children are gone. I say "ideally" because failing to prioritize memorable experiences with your spouse in addition to your children might very well ensure you won't have much of a marriage left by the time your children are grown and gone.

This is a common trap that most of us fall into from time to time. However, we cannot allow ourselves to *stay* in this trap. Your children generally will not understand this until later in life, but the best thing you can do for them is to focus on your marriage. The stronger your marriage is, the better off your children will be. There is tremendous security for a child in seeing how much their mom and dad love each other.

My son John and his wife, Kylie, do this incredibly well in their marriage using "The Four Ds":

1. **Discuss Daily:** They take ten minutes every day to talk one-on-one and check in with each other. This is not about calendaring or discussing who is picking the children up; it is about how each of them is feeling and how they can help each other carry their burdens as a team.

2. **Date Weekly:** They have a standing date night once a week. This doesn't even have to be outside the house. It might just be an intimate dinner together or a movie at home after the children go to bed.

3. **Depart Monthly:** They go somewhere together once a month. Occasionally, they splurge and have a weekend away, but mainly this is just about getting out of the house together and exploring a little bit. This could be trying out a new restaurant or going

out to a movie. The goal is not only to spend time together but also to get out of the house and away from the children and experience the world together as a couple.

4. **Dream Yearly:** They set aside some time every year to reflect back on the past year and to look ahead at the year to come. This is where they set goals and cast big visions for what they want to accomplish as a family.

These four priorities work wonders for their marriage—so much so that John and I have started to adopt them ourselves. If you aren't ready to commit to these, I'd say the bare minimum investment you should be making in your marriage is to reserve some time to *pray together, plan together, and play together*. If you aren't doing at least that, you might be risking your marriage more than you think.

Of course, you still want to be intentional about prioritizing your children above other things. While I would recommend The Four Ds for your marriage, I'd encourage you to apply "The Three Cs" to your parenting:

1. **Connect:** Find meaningful ways to connect with each child as an individual, honoring their uniqueness and who God made them to be.

2. **Care:** Show them that you care by loving them in the way they best receive love. That might be through physical touch, encouraging words, spending time together, or any other expression that speaks uniquely to them.

3. **Celebrate:** Celebrate every little victory. Too often, we save celebrations for birthdays, but there is something to celebrate every day. If they normally have cold cereal for breakfast, surprise them one day with waffles and eggs. If they ask why, just tell them you wanted to make today special. It sends them out the door with a sense that it really *can* be a special day.

Time is and will always be your most valuable resource. It's the one thing none of us can get any more of. Preserving and transferring our family values depends on us prioritizing our time in such a way that we protect our marriages, engage with our children, and create memorable experiences that will live in the minds of the next generation for the rest of their lives.

Step 5: Set the Tone

The instant you walk into a restaurant, you get an immediate feel for what kind of place it is. The lighting, music, temperature, noise level, aroma, and the way the staff is dressed tell you right from the start what to expect. It is all about the atmosphere. Those of us in the restaurant industry know you can never underestimate the power of "setting the tone" for the customer.

But what would it look like if we applied that same lens to our homes? What kind of environment or atmosphere are you trying to create for your family?

One key piece we usually get right at work but often overlook at home is the value of everyone knowing what their role or responsibility is. A nice, expensive restaurant, for instance, has a variety of different roles—several chefs, servers, host/hostess, bussers, maintenance, and management. But a quaint, mom-and-pop roadside diner might have two or three people working the whole operation. Again, all of this tells you what kind of place it is. You have different roles in your home as well. Especially in a large family, each person is going to have unique strengths, skills, and responsibilities that the others do not. When a family is working as a team, everyone knows their responsibilities and performs them well.

For example, my husband is a brilliant strategic thinker. No one I know is better at reading, research, preparation, and presenting a clear plan for adults to understand and apply. That's why he generally takes the lead in our yearly Family Assembly retreats with our adult children and their spouses. He is especially gifted at leading adults through such detailed information and training, so that's something he can "own" for us. On the other hand, I'm more naturally gifted at communicating with children and creating engaging activities for young minds. My years as a Camp Director added new tools to that gifting, so it only makes sense that I take the lead in our value experiences with our grandchildren, specifically Camp MiPa and our Assembly for Grands. With each of us operating in our strengths, John and I make a great team! We learned early in our marriage what we're each good at, and we've tried to structure our roles and experiences to match that gifting.

Another lesson from the business world we can apply at home is simply asking for feedback. It is perfectly natural at work to ask your boss how you are doing or how you could get better, but why don't we do this at home?

It can be scary to ask your children, "How am I doing as your mom? What are some things you wish I were doing differently?" There's a good chance you'll be surprised by their answer, too, just as my dad was surprised when he asked me what I'd remember most about having him as father. Of course, you cannot change your whole parenting style just to accommodate the wishes of a child, but there may be some simple things you can tweak that would mean the world to your child. If my father had asked me what I appreciated most about his parenting years earlier, for instance, I'm sure he would have made an effort to come talk to me late at night more often.

Good parents want to do the little things for their children; the problem is, we too often simply don't know *what* little things would mean the most to the child. Well ... we don't know because we don't ask. I challenge you to break that cycle and find ways to build a little self-review into your parenting as often as possible, just to make sure the investments you are making with your time and energy are the *right* investments—the ones your child really needs and responds to. When you build value experiences around what everyone is good at and what everyone needs most, you'll take those memorable experiences to the next level.

Step 6: Partner with Jesus for the Ultimate Experience

If you've gotten this far, you will no doubt create wonderful, unique, and memorable experiences for your family that will certainly preserve and transfer the family values you've identified. However, if you want to create *real* change—the kind of change that lasts forever—there's still one step left: partnering with Jesus for the ultimate experience.

As we've seen, real change starts from within. Then, you can start to work outward to bring change to your marriage, your children, and your grandchildren. But where does that personal, internal change come from?

Jesus Christ.

The psalmist declared, "Create in me a pure heart, O God, and renew a steadfast spirit within me" (Psalm 51:10, NIV). In Christ, the Father exchanges our old, sinful life for a brand-new life *with* His Son and *in* His Son: "My old self has been crucified with Christ. It is no longer I who live, but Christ lives in me. So I live in this earthly body by trusting in the Son of God, who loved me and gave himself for me" (Galatians 2:20, NLT). This doesn't just make us better people; it makes us all-new people! As the apostle Paul wrote, "This means that anyone who belongs to Christ has become a new person. The old life is gone; a new life has begun!" (2 Corinthians 5:17, NLT).

Including the Lord in your family experiences—or, better yet, building your family experiences *around* the Lord—adds an eternal dimension that ensures your family values will truly live forever. It is the Lord who put these values on your heart and in your family; these are treasures He has entrusted to your care. Only with Him and through Him can we truly preserve and transfer these values from generation to generation into eternity.

If you are walking with the Lord but haven't invited Him into your family values and experiences, I encourage you to walk back through the steps above, praying your way through the entire process. Ask Him to show you anything you've missed, anything He wants for your family that you have overlooked thus far. Be willing to change your plans, traditions, and experiences if you realize He's taking you in a different direction.

And, if you don't have a relationship with Jesus Christ, I would be remiss not to take this opportunity to encourage you to dive into the Bible and get to know Him. Talk to a Christian friend or local pastor and discover the new life Jesus is holding out to you. As Jesus Himself said, "The thief's purpose is to steal and kill and destroy. *My purpose is to give them a rich and satisfying life*" (John 10:10, NLT, emphasis added).

MAKE TODAY SPECIAL

You never know what tomorrow holds. That is why I think it is so important to be fully present in every day we've been given. As the old joke says, "Today is a gift. That's why it's called the *present.*" Especially as you get older, it is easy to fall into a rut. You can do the same things the same way with the same people every day without giving life much thought. When you do that, all the days tend to run together in your mind.

For example, many people like to talk about how "stuck" they felt in 2020 and 2021 during the COVID-19 shutdowns. Many businesses were closed, a lot of people could not go to work, and many areas had strict regulations about where you could go and who could be out and about. As a result, many people were stuck at home for months or years at a time. Men and women all over the world felt like grounded teenagers in a seemingly endless homebound imprisonment.

It seemed like the whole world fell into a rut at the same time, and that took a huge toll on people's mental and emotional well-being. Sitting here writing this in 2022, as people are finally coming out of the holes they've been in for the past two years, I'm genuinely concerned about the long-lasting effects this whole ordeal has had on us as a society. Those of us who weren't intentional about continuing to create experiences even within the limitations we have faced may find it difficult to reengage fully into life.

My prayer, especially at this unique moment in history, is that families have been awakened to the fact that we *need* fresh experiences in our lives. Without them, we can start to question everything about who we are, where we are, what we're doing, what we want out of life, and so on. Therefore, I challenge you to take this material seriously. Explore your personal and family values. Identify what they are, and then sit with them for a while, thinking and praying through how those values are reflected in your family and why they are worth preserving. Then, take seriously the call to create unique, memorable experiences that will not only *teach* but *transfer* those values to the next generation, whether as a parent or a grandparent. The children of every generation think they already have everything figured out, but you and I know what they don't: they need the wisdom and insight we've gained over a lifetime of living out these values. They need us to

transfer to them—in fun, structured, well-thought-out experiences—what we've learned through *life* experiences. And
they need us to take the lead in creating these experiences
for them.

The next generation is counting on you!

CHAPTER 10

GROWING GRAND
TOGETHER

Several of my grandchildren are extremely blessed to have meaningful memories of the time they spent with my mother, their great-grandmother. How unusual is it these days for a child to have significant memories of a great-grandparent, an elder four generations removed? How does that even happen? It happened for my family because my mother was so *intentional* as a grandparent and then later as a great-grandparent. She would sit down on the floor with the kids when they were around. She asked them questions about what was going on in their lives. She called them on the phone. She was always asking their parents how she could pray for them.

My mother was very concerned and intentional about staying connected to each individual across every generation. As a result, every one of her grandchildren and several of her great-grandchildren have wonderful memories of her. That's the kind of grandmother and great-grandmother I strive to be. But one thing I learned by watching my mother is that these connections will not happen by accident. You can't just put two people in a room and hope they form a bond—even if they're family. You need to put some work into it. As a grandparent, that means more than simply making time for your grandchildren; it also means *prioritizing* and *planning* that dedicated time with them.

PLAN YOUR TIME TOGETHER

John and I don't just *schedule* time with our grandchildren—either in groups or one-on-one. Once the time is scheduled, we are very intentional in *planning* the time we are going to spend with them. I almost never have a grandchild over to visit without a plan for how we can spend our time together. Too often, when a child spends time with a grandparent, for instance, she ends up doing the same thing at the grandparent's house that she does at her own house. The activity is the same, whether it is staring at a phone screen, watching TV, or spending time alone in a different room. The only thing that has changed is the location.

To be perfectly frank, this does nothing to deepen or enrich the emotional connection between the child and the grandparent. Why have the child over to your house at all if you aren't going to shake things up a little bit and actually make use of that time together?

Throughout this chapter, I'm going to unpack several of the tips and tricks I've used to communicate and connect with my grandchildren, but first I want to "set the stage" by stressing two things that must be top of your mind whenever and wherever you are spending quality time with your grandchildren:

1. Distraction is the enemy of connection.
2. Every interaction with a grandchild must include encouragements.

Let's dig into these just a bit.

First, it is obviously hard to connect with anyone, especially a child, if either of you is distracted. The problem is, our lives seem to be nothing *but* a constant stream of distractions! We carry around an infinite supply of second-by-second distractions in our pockets all day, every day, courtesy of our cell phones. This kills the connections we want to make with our loved ones. Just look around a restaurant the next time you're out to dinner and see how many people of all ages have their faces hidden behind a phone screen—and seniors are certainly no exception. We can struggle with the tempting buzz of a notification or the "need" to check social media just as much as anyone!

That's why we are intentional about not letting our phones interrupt something we're trying to do with anyone, especially with our children and grandchildren. Whether it's a child, a grandchild, a spouse, or anyone else, we all must work to develop the discipline needed to put our phones away and give our loved ones our full attention. They deserve it.

Today's young people were essentially born with a device in their hand, so it may be difficult for them to put them down for a period of time, but it is absolutely critical. Designate no-phone times when children are visiting. Put an empty basket on the kitchen counter and have the children drop their phones in it on their way to the dinner table. And then, of course, drop your own in there! Set smart watches to "do not disturb" and turn off the TV. The time you set aside to spend with your grandchildren is time neither of you can ever get back. None of us are getting any younger!

Second, I am a strong believer that every interaction with a grandchild must include a hearty dose of encouragement. In general, I do not think we encourage the next generation enough. It is so easy for us to point out what we don't like about the next generation, complaining about their attitude, work ethic, or whatever else has annoyed us at the moment. Our children and grandchildren don't need more complaints or criticisms. They need encouragement. We need to be more intentional about lifting them up.

And we need to be very specific in our encouragements. Don't just tell them you're proud of them. Tell them what you are proud of. Don't just say they played a good game. Point out your favorite moment from their performance. If a younger one draws you a picture, point to something specific and tell them how much you love that aspect. All these little things not only boost their confidence but show the child that you are intimately involved in their lives and that you are paying attention to the details. You aren't only interested in a surface-level relationship; you want to dive into their lives with them.

COMMUNICATING WITH YOUR GRANDCHILDREN

One way we plan time with our grandchildren is to make sure we always have conversation tools on hand wherever we are. For example, my grandson Micah loves to tell jokes. I'll occasionally buy him a joke book because he always enjoys getting new material. But I keep a joke book in the car as well. That way, when the children are in the car with me, we can pull it out and entertain one another with new jokes. I also keep conversation cards in the car and around our home. This is a great tool to help engage children in a conversation around topics you might not otherwise think of. I personally prefer using these things in the car as opposed to just handing the child a phone or iPad or installing a video player in the car. They spend enough time in front of screens as it is. When they are with me, I would rather be interacting with them.

Intentionally planning conversation tools was especially important to me recently, when we took our oldest grandchild on a trip for her seventeenth birthday. We've always had a wonderful relationship with Ashlynn, but I was honestly a bit nervous going into this trip. It was going to be just John, Ashlynn, and me for a few days, and I was worried about whether we'd be able to fill all that time with meaningful conversation. When children are young, it can seem like they never stop talking. They can go on and on and on for days. As they become teenagers, however, that often starts to taper off. Sometimes getting a teenager to talk can feel like pulling teeth! I wanted this to be a fun, relationship-building trip for all of us, and the possibility of us sitting in awkward silence for a few days got the best of me.

Instead of worrying about it or leaving it to chance, I did what I always do: I put some intentional forethought into it. I spent time thinking through some specific conversation starters tailored just for Ashlynn. Instead of using the generic conversation cards, I wanted to set up questions that matched exactly our relationship and her age. I wasn't sure if we would need them, but it made me feel so much better having them in my back pocket just in case.

Whether you're planning discussion starters ahead of time or flying by the seat of your pants, I strongly recommend getting in the habit of asking *open-ended* questions. After working with so many children professionally as a Camp Director, volunteering as a Children's Ministry Coordinator in our local church, and now as a very active grandmother, I have learned the immense value of asking children open-ended questions. Too often, if you ask a child a question that can be answered with either yes or no, they will only answer with a yes or a no. Learning how to ask open-ended questions, however, can make your conversations ten times more meaningful. For example, instead of asking a child, "Did you have a nice day?" you might say, "Tell me two really funny things that happened at school today." This one simple change in how you phrase questions can open new worlds of conversation and add a fresh depth and dimension to your relationships.

CONNECTING WITH YOUR GRANDCHILDREN

Oftentimes, there's a wide cultural, communication, and/or spiritual gap between grandparents and grandchildren simply because we do not know how to relate to them and their interests. I'll never be able to play video games very well, for instance, but that doesn't stop me from grabbing a controller and playing (poorly) when they ask me to!

The key to bridging these gaps is, once again, intentionality. Can you tell that intentionality is one of my key focuses in everything I do? Success never happens by accident. You can either plan for it or wait for it—but if you decide to wait, you will wait a *looooong* time. As a grandparent, I want to plan for successful relationships with my grandchildren by making the best of the time we share. Some of the ways John and I do this are:

Playing Together

The best, most effective, most enjoyable, most bond-building thing we do with our grandchildren is simply playing together. We play outside, play board games, do puzzles, play card games, cook, do crafts, go fishing, visit amusement parks, and so on. We spent the previous two chapters discussing some of the bigger experiences you can establish in your family, but never underestimate the power and lasting significance of smaller, daily shared experiences. That's how you "do life" together, and it creates momentum in your family.

I know that not all of us are wired to "play," and as we get older, there are often physical limitations that prevent us from doing everything we might otherwise want to do with our grandchildren. I realize that my children and grandchildren were very blessed to have my mother—their grandmother or great-grandmother—who remained strong and healthy well into her nineties. She had a treadmill she used to walk three miles a day on throughout her eighties, and then she switched to riding a recumbent bicycle in her nineties! That focus on her health helped give her the energy to take long walks or sit on the floor with her "great-grands." I'm pretty fortunate healthwise myself, and I'm able to run around with the children a good bit. But I know that isn't always the case. We're all getting older, and that, sadly, often puts a damper on our play time.

However, there is always something you can do to play with your grandchildren. Even if you have limited mobility, you can probably sit at the kitchen table and play board games or card games. Most children aren't expecting their grandparents to play paintball or go dirt bike racing with them! Don't worry about what you *can't* do; just focus on what you *can*. If that means going head-to-head in a mean game of Monopoly, go for it! The value is in the time and experience you're sharing, not merely the type of activity. Whatever you choose or are able to play, the key is that you are not just sitting around watching time go by; you are actively engaged in your life and your family. You are *going somewhere*, and you are going there *together*.

Let Them Teach You Something

A great way to bridge the generation gap with a child is to let them teach you something. So often, we get this attitude that we as adults know everything, and we think children have nothing to teach us. That is far from the truth! When I get my eight-year-old grandchild to show me how to do something on my phone, it creates a wonderful bonding moment. It makes him feel very confident about the fact that he's helping a grown-up, and he gets this rush of healthy pride that he was able to teach me something important.

Similarly, some of our children have such complicated home entertainment setups that I'd have no idea how to even turn on the television if I wanted to. Rather than fumbling around with the two or three remote controls sitting on the coffee table, I'd rather take advantage of the opportunity to have a young grandchild do it for me. Again, they probably know which buttons to push, and it gives them the chance to teach Mimi something.

As I've said, today's children were practically born with a device in their hand, so using all these new gadgets comes naturally to them. More importantly, most children don't have the intimidation around technology that many adults have. Use that to your advantage in building a connection with them!

Share Music, Movies, and TV Shows

Another great connection point with your grandchildren can revolve around sharing music, movies, and TV shows.

John and I spend a few days together in the mountains with our older grandchildren—those thirteen years and older—every year. On the drive up, we create our playlist for the weekend. I will start by creating a new playlist on my phone and adding three or four of my favorite songs. Then I will pass my phone to one of the grandchildren and have them do the same. We keep passing my phone around until everyone has had a chance to throw a few songs onto the playlist, and that becomes our playlist for the weekend.

They always laugh when one of John's or my picks from the seventies or eighties comes on. It's a good chance for us to remind them that their children will one day laugh at their music too! We also use their music selections to get to know them a little better. We'll ask, "What do you like about this song?" It gives us a chance to get a close look at some unique aspects of their personality, and it helps us appreciate each grandchild as an individual.

While we don't watch a lot of television, we will sit down to watch a movie or TV show with them occasionally. When they share one of their favorite shows with us, we will ask them to explain what they like about it and how it makes them feel. If the program portrays some kind of moral issue or tense situation, we might have a conversation later about what they would have done in that situation or how they felt the characters in the show handled themselves. This gives us a chance to pull some extra value out of time we might otherwise have spent mindlessly watching a screen.

Learn the Lingo

This might seem like a silly point, but I try to stay at least a little up to date with the current slang and idioms that today's young people are using. There is an almost fifty-year age gap between my oldest grandchild and me. That means there is a huge *language* gap between that generation and me. They use terms every day that I've never heard before. It may not feel natural, but I take some effort to stay up to date with their lingo just so I can comfortably communicate with them.

For example, I've heard my oldest grandchild, Ashlynn, call her father *bruh* quite a bit. Honestly, it sounded a little disrespectful to me at first . . . until I saw how her dad, Trent, said it back to her. This silly little term, which basically means *friend,* has become a term of endearment for them. The fact that Ashlynn feels so comfortable calling her father that—and the fact that he's comfortable *allowing* her to call him that—is kind of sweet to me now.

Other terms I've had to learn in recent years include *peep* (short for *people,* meaning "*friends*"), YOLO ("you only live once"), FOMO ("fear of missing out"), *yeet* (to throw something), *chill* (calm down), *bounce* (to leave in a hurry), *salty* (angry), and GOAT ("greatest of all time"). Now, do I use my new expanded vocabulary when I'm talking to my husband, friends, and coworkers? Absolutely not! But it's nice to be able to "translate" what my grandchildren are saying!

Pray for Them

Of everything I do with and for my grandchildren, I firmly believe the most important thing is to pray for them—and

John and I do this a *lot*. Sometimes, people develop an attitude about prayer, as though prayer isn't *enough*. We might even apologize when we feel like "all we can do is pray." But prayer is the single most important thing we can do for our children and grandchildren! It is literally going to the Creator of the universe, the throne room of Almighty God, and asking Him to show favor and blessing to someone you love. How can we ever diminish that as "all we can do"?

One of our grandsons just had a birthday this past week, and John and I spent some time in prayer for this young man. We went to the throne of God on his behalf, using his name in prayer, asking for God to be with him and shape him over this next important time in his life. Praying for any individual by name is powerful, but there's something extra special about praying for your own child or grandchild by name, especially when you can do this in their presence. I think there's a unique bond any time one generation in the family prays specifically for another.

We are also constantly asking our children how we can pray for them and their children. Each of us is always dealing with our own unique set of circumstances and challenges. That is true for adults, and it is certainly true for children of all ages. So, don't stop at general prayers for growth and well-being. Be specific. Dig into their lives, find out what they are concerned about, and focus your prayers on those areas. As Scripture says, "The earnest prayer of a righteous person has great power and produces wonderful results" (James 5:16, NLT).

GRANDPARENTING FROM A DISTANCE

Until recently, two of my four children's families lived out of state from us. That means John and I have been physically separated from several grandchildren for most of their lives. However, we wanted to be just as present for those out-of-town grandchildren as we were for the ones who lived nearby. This is an extremely common situation for grandparents—being physically separated from the children for long stretches of time. Fortunately, we live in a time when transportation and communication are relatively cheap and accessible. Here are some things we did to close the physical gap between us and our grandchildren when we were apart.

Be as Physically Present as You Can

Whenever one of our out-of-town children's family invited us to visit with them for a weekend, holiday, or special occasion, we tried to make it if at all possible so we could be physically present with them for a little while. Typically, that was around an event like a soccer game or some special occasion that was already planned that they wanted us to be a part of. There's just no substitute for physically being there.

Traveling to visit your family also gives you the benefit of staying in their home overnight. That's a much more intimate setting because you are actually "doing life" with them for however long you are there. That means you see them when you wake up, you have breakfast together, you spend the day together, and you see one another all the way up to bedtime. To go from being in different cities to being under the same roof for a few days makes the whole experience much more significant and meaningful.

For example, one of our family's favorite Christmas memories is the year our first grandchild was born. My daughter Joy and her husband, Trent, lived in Fort Payne, Alabama, at the time, which was about two and a half hours from our home in Atlanta. Our granddaughter was born a few weeks before Christmas, so their little family didn't feel like spending the holidays away from their new (and important) routine at home with the baby. Instead, they invited John, our other three children (all unmarried at the time), and me to spend Christmas with them in their home. It was such a special and memorable Christmas for our entire family. We all got a lot of one-on-one time with the baby, Joy and Trent got plenty of rest, and we all enjoyed "living" together again for a few days.

That Christmas, we all got up, celebrated Christmas morning together in the living room, gushed over the baby's first Christmas, ate all three meals together in the house, and played games all day and night. We never even changed out of pajamas all day! It was a warm, wonderful holiday memory that we'll always cherish. A big reason for this is that John and I weren't "in charge." We were in our daughter and son-in-law's home, participating in *their* holiday and enjoying *their* hospitality. We got to experience the joy of being *hosted* by our daughter and son-in-law, and being present with them in that new way was a joy.

Use Technology

There's a stereotype about technology and those of us who are old enough to be grandparents—and it may or may not be well deserved. Sure, there are some grandmas and grandpas who struggle to make sense of their cell phones and computers, but I'd argue there are just as many of us who are quite proud of how far we've come in so short a time. The world has changed quite a bit since I was born in 1955, and frankly, I'm pretty happy with how well I've kept up!

The advances could not have come at a better time as far as I'm concerned. Easy access to video calling through FaceTime, Zoom, and other common tools has revolutionized grandparenting. My children spent most of their childhood in Brazil, thousands of miles away from their grandparents. The only times my children ever got to engage with their grandparents face-to-face were the rare times we were either in the States or when their grandparents came to visit us. I would have loved for my children to have had easy, inexpensive access to my parents, face-to-face, whenever they wanted, but the technology wasn't there yet. Today, it is.

If you have grandchildren and haven't yet experimented with all these wonderful new tools, I strongly encourage you to at least dip your toe in the technology waters. Besides the video-calling applications that are available (on the devices you probably already own), you can engage in one-on-one and group chats with your grandchildren, participate in online photo albums, set up a shared family calendar showing everyone's key events, and even attend key sporting or school events remotely. There's a good chance your grandchild's school is already streaming their sporting events and graduations live online for free. These live, remote streaming options are commonplace these days, especially in our post-COVID world.

Personal home assistants, such as Amazon's Echo (Alexa) devices, even make direct video calling drop-dead simple and hands-free. Once it's set up, all you have to do is say, "Alexa, call <name>," and you're instantly connected to your loved one via a crystal clear video call. It's almost unbelievable for those of us who grew up with only a single landline telephone mounted to the kitchen wall!

If you aren't taking advantage of all the new features modern technology has to offer, you're missing out on some key grandparenting opportunities!

Send Cards, Texts, and Random Notes of Encouragement

As I mentioned in chapter 6, I am a huge fan of sending cards for different occasions. Of course, that extends to birthday cards for the grandchildren. Every grandchild always gets a handwritten birthday card from me, no matter where they live. I've had grandchildren living literally right next door to me, and I still wrote them a card.

I've also tried to stay up to date with what is going on in their lives. We work hard to maintain a family calendar that shows everyone's sporting events, school events, church activities, social milestones, and so on. That way, when I know someone has a soccer game coming up, I can call or send a text or note that says, "I know you have a game coming up. I'm looking forward to hearing all about it afterward." Then I try to remember to follow up with them to let them know I haven't forgotten.

Most of my grandchildren are too young to have phones of their own yet, but I maintain text strings with the ones who do. That definitely makes things easier. For the younger ones who don't have phones, I have to be a lot more disciplined in my note writing. If one of them ever draws a picture and gives it to me when we're together, for instance, I'll always try to follow up the next week with a thank-you note telling them how much I appreciated that gift. This does a few things. First, it gives me another connection point with that child. Second, hopefully it makes them feel good about the gift they gave me. Third, it gives me an opportunity to teach them by example how to express gratitude, as I discussed in chapter 6.

The bottom line with all these tools and practices is that, whether the child is near or far geographically, I am always trying to stay aware of what activities they are involved in and how I can participate in and even contribute to their life.

BE AVAILABLE TO TALK (BUT DON'T BE OFFENDED IF/WHEN THEY GO TO SOMEONE ELSE)

Children of all ages need someone to talk to. And, as we've all learned, that person will often not be the parent or grandparent. Many parents and grandparents get a little jealous about this. They've invested so much into their child's life for so long, it can be hard to accept the reality that the child may simply need a different perspective or feels safer going to someone else with a particular issue. I have faced that as a child, as a parent, and now as a grandparent. As much as we would love to be the be-all and end-all resource for the children of our lives, that's just not how it goes. Therefore, you want to have godly, like-minded people in your child's life who they can go to with difficult questions or situations when they don't want to talk to you about it—*and* you have to give them freedom to do so.

Just this morning as I write this, my daughter Joy told me about a conversation she'd had with her eleven-year-old son, Daniel. Apparently, Daniel had heard something in the sermon the previous week at church that he had been wrestling with a bit. He came to his mother and said, "Mom, the pastor said *this* last week, I've got some questions about it. I think I'm going to talk to him about it when I see him this Sunday."

Now, could he have asked his mother his questions? Of course. But he's getting a little older now, and he chose to discuss it with another adult. Because their family has built a great relationship with their pastor, Daniel feels comfortable going straight to the pastor with his questions. I imagine there are some parents who would say, "Oh, I'm sure the pastor has more important things to do than discuss this with a child. Why don't you just ask me, and we'll see if we can figure it out together?"

That may seem like a nice offer to help and personally engage with the child, but what it really does is send a message that the pastor is too busy to deal with questions from the congregation—especially a child. From all the pastors I've known and worked with over the years, I know this is not the case. I am proud that Joy respected her son's relationship with the pastor enough to step aside. She sent their pastor a text that simply said, "FYI: Daniel has a few questions about your sermon last week. He said he would rather talk about it with you, so he'll probably ask you about it this week."

That is such a healthy attitude for a parent. But I know it is possible only because they've worked hard to develop a good relationship with their church leaders and because they've helped their children feel comfortable going to others, which includes their network of godly adults.

Along these lines, if the child *does* choose to come to you as the parent or grandparent, you need to see that for what it is: a tremendous honor. Give that child your full attention, provide value for the trust they've placed in you, and express gratitude for the fact that they came to you with this issue.

Just about the worst thing you can do when a child or grandchild comes to you with something troubling or personal is to overreact. When a child comes home and shares something with you that completely rocks your world and you never expected to hear, you have to discipline yourself to keep your reaction in check. If you blow up at them or make them feel embarrassed for raising the issue, they may never come to you again. A better response is to take a deep breath and say, "Thank you for sharing that with me. Tell me more." The goal should be to keep the dialogue going, and even a slight overreaction on your part can shut it down.

THE FIRM FOUNDATION

Obviously, I love being a grandparent. In many ways, it has brought my lifelong journey full-circle. That little girl who grew up dreaming about raising a big family has seen her dreams come true. I always knew my children would be an enormous blessing, but what I didn't know way back then was how amazing the *second* blessing would be when I became a grandmother—sixteen times over!

The values we've lived by for the past forty-five years—and the values my parents lived by before then—have led us into a full, rich family life that has exceeded my wildest expectations. God has been so good. Brick by brick, He has built a blessed life for us. The Lord—and the values He's instilled within us—have become our family's firm foundation.

The foundation is critical for any building.

When the Chick-fil-A Support Center was under construction, our family would often stop by to see the progress. I recall seeing that foundation soon after it was laid; it was massive. But the size of the foundation must meet the demands of the building. Since this was going to be a five-story building, it required a large foundation.

Construction was completed years ago, and today, whenever I walk into that building, I can't see the foundation. I never even think about it. But it's there, sitting just below the surface. Every wall, every window, every elevator, cubicle, conference room, footstep, and coffeepot in every break room *depends* on that foundation every second of every day. Without it, the entire structure—and everything and everyone in it—would collapse.

Everything that is seen is the result of the unseen. When you look at a tree, you don't see the roots—but you know they're there, firmly grounding and nourishing the whole tree. When you fly a kite, you don't see the wind—but you know it's there, lifting and supporting the weight of the kite, enabling it to soar. When I look at my grandchildren, I can't see my parents—but I know they're there, the legacy of their values shaping the emotional and spiritual development of the next generation, many of whom never even knew my parents.

The foundation is critical for any family.

The psalmist declared, "Unless the Lord *builds* a house, the work of the builders is wasted" (Psalm 127:1, NLT, emphasis added). The apostle Paul rejoiced, "For we are God's *masterpiece*. He has created us anew in Christ Jesus, so we can do the good things he planned for us long ago" (Ephesians 2:10, NLT, emphasis added). The Lord is *building* our lives, and He is *building* our families. And I believe the pillars He uses to set those foundations are our values—the essentials, the nonnegotiables, the very cornerstone of who He made each of us to be and what He has called each of us to do.

On that foundation, He can build a magnificent home for you and your family. He *wants* to. Proverbs says, "By wisdom a house is built, and through understanding it is established; through knowledge its rooms are filled with rare and beautiful treasures" (Proverbs 24:3–4, NIV). The rarest and most beautiful treasures in my home by far have been my children and grandchildren.

John and I are in our midsixties. We are as active as ever, but only God knows how much longer we have on earth to live out our values in front of our children and grandchildren and to help guide them as they grow more and more into the wonderfully unique individuals God has created them to be. I suppose that's why I feel a bit of urgency in making the most of every moment with them—and why you've heard me use the word *intentional* so often in this book. I even sign my emails with "Intentionally Influencing, Trudy Cathy White." Because that's what I'm trying to do with my life: to be intentional and purposeful in how, when, and where I use the influence God has given me. In no other area of my life is that more important than in the time I spend with my family—living out our values and seeking God's will for our lives.

God has been so faithful to us, just as He's been faithful to you. And that faithfulness brings with it a serious responsibility:

> Just make sure you stay alert. Keep close watch over yourselves. Don't forget anything of what you've seen. Don't let your heart wander off. Stay vigilant as long as you live. Teach what you've seen and heard to your children and grandchildren. (Deuteronomy 4:9, MSG)

We must *remember* what God has done for us. And we must *pass it on* to our children and grandchildren. As John and I often remind ourselves, "The legacy you leave *then* is the life you are living *now*." Of all the wonderful, challenging callings God has put on my life, this is the one I most want to "get right." And this is the one I'll think about, pray about, and work on every day I have left on earth.

Fortunately, it's also the one that has brought me the most joy.

That is my prayer for you too. I pray God's richest blessings on you as you take what we've discussed in this book and make it a reality in your family.

Identify your values.

Preserve them.

Transfer them.

That is how you truly leave a legacy on this earth and, more importantly, in the hearts and minds of the people you love the most—the ones who will carry your values into future generations.

> *But from everlasting to everlasting*
> *the LORD's love is with those who fear him,*
> *and his righteousness with their children's children—*
> *with those who keep his covenant*
> *and remember to obey his precepts.*
> —Psalm 103:17–18, NIV

PERSONAL VALUES CARD SORT

Make a copy of the *Personal Values Card Sort* on the following pages, cut each card out, and follow the instructions in chapter 2 to walk your family through the values card exercise.[5]

Personal Values Card Sort

William R. Miller, Janet C'de Baca Daniel
B. Matthews & Paula Wilbourne

University of New Mexico, 2011

Designed for Avery 5371
Business Card Template

The Personal Values Card Sort is in the
public domain and may be copied or
adapted without further permission.

Not Important to Me

Somewhat Important to Me

Important to Me

Very Important to Me

Most Important to Me

Other value:

Other value:

Other value:

ACCEPTANCE to be accepted as I am 1	**ACCURACY** to be correct in my opinions and beliefs 2
ACHIEVEMENT to have important accomplishments 3	**ADVENTURE** to have new and exciting experiences 4
ART to appreciate or express myself in art 5	**ATTRACTIVENESS** to be physically attractive 6
AUTHORITY to be in charge of others 7	**AUTONOMY** to be self-determined and independent 8
BEAUTY to appreciate beauty around me 9	**BELONGING** to have a sense of belonging, being part of 10

CARING to take care of others 11	**CHALLENGE** to take on difficult tasks and problems 12
COMFORT to have a pleasant and comfortable life 13	**COMMITMENT** to make enduring, meaningful commitments 14
COMPASSION to feel and act on concern for others 15	**COMPLEXITY** to embrace the intricacies of life 16
COMPROMISE to be willing to give and take in reaching agreements 17	**CONTRIBUTION** to make a lasting contribution in the world 18
COOPERATION to work collaboratively with others 19	**COURAGE** to be brave and strong in the face of adversity 20

COURTESY

to be considerate and polite toward others

21

CREATIVITY

to create new things or ideas

22

CURIOSITY

to seek out, experience and learn new things

23

DEPENDABILITY

to be reliable and trustworthy

24

DILIGENCE

to be thorough and conscientious in whatever I do

25

DUTY

to carry out my duties and obligations

26

ECOLOGY

to live in harmony with the environment

27

EXCITEMENT

to have a life full of thrills and stimulation

28

FAITHFULNESS

to be loyal and true in relationships

29

FAME

to be known and recognized

30

FAMILY to have a happy, loving family 31	**FITNESS** to be physically fit and strong 32
FLEXIBILITY to adjust to new circumstances easily 33	**FORGIVENESS** to be forgiving of others 34
FREEDOM to be free from undue restric- tions and limitations 35	**FRIENDSHIP** to have close, supportive friends 36
FUN to play and have fun 37	**GENEROSITY** to give what I have to others 38
GENUINENESS to act in a manner that is true to who I am 39	**GOD'S WILL** to seek and obey the will of God 40

GRATITUDE to be thankful and appreciative 41	**GROWTH** to keep changing and growing 42
HEALTH to be physically well and healthy 43	**HONESTY** to be honest and truthful 44
HOPE to maintain a positive and optimistic outlook 45	**HUMILITY** to be modest and unassuming 46
HUMOR to see the humorous side of myself and the world 47	**IMAGINATION** to have dreams and see possibilities 48
INDEPENDENCE to be free from depending on others 49	**INDUSTRY** to work hard and well at my life tasks 50

INNER PEACE

to experience personal peace

51

INTEGRITY

to live my daily life in a way that
is consistent with my values

52

INTELLIGENCE

to keep my mind sharp and active

53

INTIMACY

to share my innermost experiences with others

54

JUSTICE

to promote fair and equal treatment for all

55

KNOWLEDGE

to learn and contribute valuable knowledge

56

LEADERSHIP

to inspire and guide others

57

LEISURE

to take time to relax and enjoy

58

LOVED

to be loved by those close to me

59

LOVING

to give love to others

60

MASTERY to be competent in my everyday activities 61	**MINDFULNESS** to live conscious and mindful of the present moment 62
MODERATION To avoid excesses and find a middle ground 63	**MONOGAMY** to have one close, loving relationship 64
MUSIC to enjoy or express myself in music 65	**NON-CONFORMITY** to question and challenge authority and norms 66
NOVELTY to have a life full of change and variety 67	**NURTURANCE** to encourage and support others 68
OPENNESS to be open to new experi- ences, ideas and options 69	**ORDER** to have a life that is well ordered and organized 70

PASSION

to have deep feelings about
ideas, activities or people

71

PATRIOTISM

to love, serve and protect my country

72

PLEASURE

to feel good

73

POPULARITY

to be well liked by many people

74

POWER

to have control over others

75

PRACTICALITY

to focus on what is practical,
prudent, and sensible

76

PROTECT

to protect and keep safe those I love

77

PROVIDE

to provide for and take care of my family

78

PURPOSE

to have meaning and direction in my life

79

RATIONALITY

to be guided by reason, logic and evidence

80

REALISM to see and act realistically and practically 81	**RESPONSIBILITY** to make and carry out responsible decisions 82
RISK to take risks and chances 83	**ROMANCE** to have intense, exciting love in my life 84
SAFETY to be safe and secure 85	**SELF-ACCEPTANCE** to accept myself as I am 86
SELF-CONTROL to be disciplined in my own actions 87	**SELF-ESTEEM** to feel good about myself 88
SELF-KNOWLEDGE to have a deep and honest understanding of myself 89	**SERVICE** to be helpful and of service to others 90

SEXUALITY

to have an active and satisfying sex life

91

SIMPLICITY

to live life simply, with minimal needs

92

SOLITUDE

to have time and space where
I can be apart from others

93

SPIRITUALITY

to grow and mature spiritually

94

STABILITY

to have a life that stays fairly consistent

95

TOLERANCE

to accept and respect those
who differ from me

96

TRADITION

to follow respected patterns of the past

97

VIRTUE

to live a morally pure and excellent life

98

WEALTH

to have plenty of money

99

WORLD PEACE

to work to promote peace in the world

100

FAMILY ASSEMBLY:
AGENDA AND DISCUSSION POINTS

Every year, we spend one weekend with our adult children and their spouses in our annual Family Assembly. We generally go to a mountain cabin or retreat to get away from all distractions, and we always prepare an agenda beforehand. While all of us grown-ups enjoy the time away together, and although we do plan some free time activities, this retreat is certainly not a vacation. This is a dedicated time once a year in which we all come together to learn, grow, and steward our family business—both personal and professional.

We mostly stick to the five broad topics below, and I've provided some subtopics to demonstrate how we dig into each area. As you implement a Family Assembly of your own, feel free to select any of these topics and subtopics and flesh

them out according to the interests of your own family and
your adult children's families.

Relationships

- Updates from individuals
- Praying for each family member by name and
  specific needs

Estate Planning

- Philanthropy
- Education
- Communication/clarity

Business Planning

- Corporate and social responsibility
- Current affairs, issues, and challenges
- Prayer time for the business's specific needs
- Ownership responsibility
- Education

Personal Development

- Finances and stewardship
- Spiritual nourishment
- Values
- Marriage enrichment

Fun

- Board games and/or card games
- Outings
- Family meals prepared by couples as assigned

APPENDIX

ASSEMBLY FOR GRANDS: GRANDPARENT/GRANDCHILD ANNUAL RETREAT GUIDE

Every year, we spend one weekend with our grandchildren aged thirteen and up in our Assembly for Grands, which grew out of our annual Family Assembly that we have with our adult children and their spouses. This is a special weekend we spend with our older, teenage grandchildren without their parents, where we have the opportunity to speak into their lives and help prepare them for the responsibilities ahead of them as members of the family.

Just like the Family Assembly we have with their parents, this weekend is well planned and, while it includes plenty of fun activities, the main goal is to help guide our grandchildren as they mature into the Christ-centered young men and women God made them to be. We do this by focusing on the key issues outlined below, and we typically include an additional focus or self-discovery tool such as Tom Rath's *StrengthsFinder*, Gary Chapman's *The Five Love Languages*, and Rick Warren's *The Purpose Driven Life*.

Review the topics outlined below and feel free to adapt and add to them as necessary according to the specific needs of your teen grandchildren.

Moral Development

The first area of development we target is *moral development*, or helping the next generation learn to make ethical decisions in difficult situations, especially as they develop in their adolescent years. We believe in teaching the next generation to make ethical and moral decisions in regard to their family, trusted friends, outside mentors, people of influence in their lives, and, of course, their own biblical worldview.

The best lab for teaching the next generation moral development is their own life, helping them through the *process of decision-making* as they face adolescent difficulties. You can do this by doing the following:

- Helping them *develop good questions* to ask of themselves when they face a difficult decision.
- Moving their ethical and moral decision-making from *external* (what others would think) to more *internal* (what they believe) motivation through a series of questions that help filter their decisions through their biblical worldview.

- Teaching them that wise decision-making is not based on guilt or the expectations of others but on their understanding of Scripture and a high character development in themselves.

One of the most important building blocks in this moral development is the *ability to have empathy for others*. This will help them see things not from their own point of view but from the other point of view.

Etiquette Development

Another area is *etiquette development*, which gives teens confidence in interacting with others in a formal setting. When young people know how to dress, speak, and act around peers, dates, adults, teachers, and leaders, they not only develop a reputation for maturity and showing respect but they feel better about themselves and relieve the anxiety many teens feel in different social and professional situations as well. Specific areas of etiquette we target include the following:

- **Table Etiquette:** You can set a fancy table decked out with every piece of silverware that could possibly be on the table and teach which utensil is proper to use with what dish. Also instruct them how to use their napkin, how to properly hold utensils, how to remove a bite of food from their mouth when necessary, and so on. Having these basic skills will give them a great sense of confidence, especially as they begin dating and/or having more meals away from home.

- **Cell Phone Etiquette:** By adolescence, children should practice cell phone etiquette, which includes setting a cell phone to vibrate when in public or with others, putting the phone away while eating at the table, not being distracted by a phone while talking to someone else in person, not using speakerphone in public, and conducting both text and voice conversations in private.
- **Greeting Etiquette:** Ensure that the next generation understands that properly greeting someone includes smiling, making eye contact, shaking hands, and staying engaged in the conversation.
- **Gift Etiquette:** Explain that proper gift etiquette involves expressing gratitude by texting or writing thank-you notes promptly when someone sends a gift.
- **Computer Etiquette:** Computer etiquette includes communicating respectfully with others, despite the lack of face-to-face contact—especially on social media. This should also include clear discussions about how *not* to let someone else's negative comments affect their own self-esteem and how to avoid basing their self-worth on the number of "likes" their social media activity gets. Demonstrate proper etiquette and respectful behavior for your teens in daily life to help them learn from your example.
- **Speaking Etiquette:** Practice standing up tall, voice projection, and exercises to eliminate stuttering and stammering with unnecessary words such as *uh, um,* and *you know.*

Business Development

A third area, especially if your family owns or helps lead a company, is *business development*. As early as possible, provide a hands-on experience at the lowest level of the business that will help the next generation connect with the importance of the business. For example, we want each of our next generation of family members to understand the purpose of why we are in business and the value we place on people. So, they are challenged to memorize and understand Chick-fil-A's purpose statement and to have a working knowledge of key leadership positions and people.

Even if you don't own and operate a family business, you can still help prepare the next generation of professionals by instructing them on things like the following:

- Governance and organizational structure, such as a board of directors, governance, management, and shareholders
- Strategy planning
- Finance and accounting
- Economy and free enterprise (supply chain, retail, construction, real estate, etc.)
- Sales, marketing, and branding

The investments you make in your teen grandchild's life today will pay huge dividends when they enter the workforce, so try to think twenty years into their future and help prepare them to become the kind of employees and leaders you want them to be.

APPENDIX

CAMP MIPA: GRANDPARENT/GRANDCHILD SUMMER CAMP GUIDE

I n the summer of 2017, we held the first of what immediately became an annual event with all our grandchildren (who are out of diapers): Camp MiPa, a three-day/night summer camp experience. The name "Camp MiPa" comes from our grandparent names, Mimi and Papa. We go all out every year, filling the days and nights with games, Bible studies, group activities, and plenty of time for all the grandchildren to interact with one another and with us. As with all our family events, we take this very seriously and plan it with great *attention* and *intention*.

If you'd like to try holding your own special summer camp with your grandchildren, here are a few tips to get you started.

Plan a Schedule

Our camp is a full three days and nights, but you can make yours however long you want: one day, two days, a long weekend, or even a few half days like a Vacation Bible School experience. Whatever you decide, be sure to spend plenty of time scheduling the days just as intentionally as if you were planning a VBS for your church.

Pray for Opportunity

This is a chance for you to influence the next generation through the creative use of your time. The goal is to make a lifelong investment in their character and spiritual growth. Be sure to bathe every opportunity in prayer, asking the Lord to guide you in every detail, activity, and conversation.

Identify a Theme

Decide on a particular topic of focus and build your experiences around that theme. For example, I mentioned earlier in the book that one of our themes was "So, So Good." Our key Scripture passage was Psalm 34:8, "Taste and see that the Lord is good; blessed is the one who takes refuge in him" (NIV). In that spirit, we crafted many of our activities around the theme of cooking and tasting. This included things like cook-off competitions, baking lessons, chef hats, a playlist of songs about God's goodness, and so on.

Identify Fun Language

This should be a special event for you and your grandchildren, so go the extra mile by using creative language for common things. For example, our grandchildren sleep in bedrooms in our home, but we don't call them *bedrooms*; we call them *bunkhouses*. They don't have *roommates*; they have *bunkmates*. We don't have *cousins* and *grandchildren*; we have *campers*. Sometimes these terms can be based on your theme, and other times they can be based on general camp terminology. The idea here is to make this truly feel like a camp experience and not just a normal weekend at Grandma and Grandpa's house

Create a Team Culture

Create camaraderie among your campers by having everyone wear the same color T-shirt or even creating your own camp T-shirts for them. Group them by ages or by intentionally mixing the ages, and let the older campers help out the younger ones. Let the campers create chants for their team, and assign responsibilities by team for helping with cooking, serving meals, and cleaning up.

Design Activities

Plan your activities around general camp culture. This could include plenty of outside play, indoor crafts, daily devotions, music, drama with simple costumes, free time, rest time, snack time, cabin cleanup, and so on.

Boost Confidence and Character

Be intentional about creating confidence and building character with the camp rules, award ceremonies, and unity cheers. For example, we have:

H.O.G. Award

We offer a reward each day for the camper(s) who show kindness and care to other campers. We call this the H.O.G. (Helping Others Grow) Award, and it includes a special necklace they can wear all day at camp.

- **Camp Rules:** Our primary rule for all campers, which we repeat often, is "Thoughts positive, words encouraging, hands helping."
- **Camp Purpose:** The clear focus of our camp experience—the whole reason John and I go to so much trouble—is summed up in the title of chapter 10: Growing Grand Together.
- **Camp Cheer:** We even came up with a little cheer that we recite as a group throughout our days and nights at camp: "I say 'growing,' you say 'grand': Growing (Grand)! Growing (Grand)! I say 'to' you say 'gether': To (gether)! To (gether)! Camp MiPa, hey!"

Notes

1   Adapted from W. R. Miller, J. C'de Baca, D. B. Matthews, and P. L. Wilbourne, *Personal Values Card Sort,* University of New Mexico, 2001. Full tool provided in the appendix of this book.

2   C. T. Studd, "Only One Life, 'Twill Soon Be Past."

3   Ron Blue, *God Owns It All* (Nashville: LifeWay, 2016), 78.

4   Alan Fadling, *An Unhurried Life: Following Jesus' Rhythms of Work and Rest* (Downers Grove: IVP Books, 2013), 64.

5   Miller, C'de Baca, Matthews, and Wilbourne, *Personal Values Card Sort.*

About the Author

Trudy Cathy White is a native Georgian and the only daughter of Jeannette and S. Truett Cathy, the founder of Chick-fil-A, Inc. An ambassador for the family business, Trudy has held various roles within Chick-fil-A, including that of restaurant operator at just 19 years old.

Trudy and her husband, John, served as missionaries in Brazil and co-founded Lifeshape and Impact 360 Institute. A developer and encourager at heart, White served as the Director of WinShape Camps for Girls from 2003-2017. She is a speaker, author, dedicated wife, mother of four, and grandmother of sixteen. Every day, she is fueled by her passion to be intentional with her influence.

In everything Trudy does, she is led by her commitment to obey God's leadership, nurture family relationships, and promote godly character in the next generation.

If you enjoyed *A Legacy that Lasts,* don't miss these other Forefront Books titles by Trudy Cathy White.

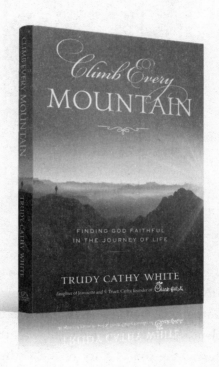

In *Climb Every Mountain,* Trudy Cathy White invites you to join her on an expedition toward, up, and over the mountains most of us face in life—challenges such as figuring out our identity in Christ, understanding the gifts and calling God's given us, godly parenting, and leaving (and living) a legacy for others to follow.

Chick-fil-A has become a national phenomenon over the past fifty years, forever changing the fast-food industry in terms of food quality and customer service. Much has been written about Chick-fil-A founder S. Truett Cathy over the years, but the true, behind-the-scenes story of the Cathy family has never been told...until now.

In *A Quiet Strength*, Truett's daughter, Trudy Cathy White, tells the story of the real heart and soul of the Cathy family: her mother, Jeannette M. Cathy.

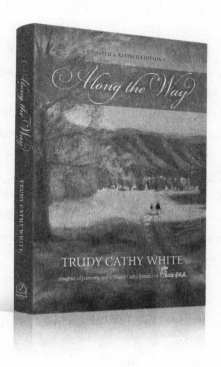

Along the Way is the inspiring true story of Trudy Cathy White from her childhood to adulthood, her years in Brazil as a missionary, and the many lessons she's learned "along the way."

About Impact 360® Institute

Impact 360 Institute has been cultivating leaders who follow Jesus since 2006. Through biblical worldview education, community-based discipleship, leadership coaching, vocational mentoring, and missional opportunities, students are equipped to live as change-agents in the world.

Impact 360 Institute serves High School graduates through their nine-month Impact 360 Fellows experience, teenagers for one and two weeks through Impact 360 Immersion and Propel, and young professionals through Impact 360 Residency.

About the Impact 360 Legacy Grant Fund

All proceeds from the sale of this book will support the students at Impact 360 Institute through the Legacy Grant Fund. The Impact 360 Legacy Grant Fund provides need-based financial aid to families. Our desire is to make this program possible for any young leader. Join us as we Cultivate Leaders Who Follow Jesus!

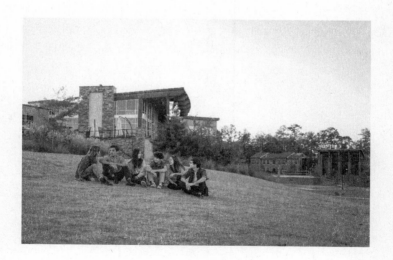